REMEMBER ME!

**FROM GRADUATION TO LANDING YOUR FIRST JOB
HOW TO LAUNCH YOUR CAREER**

MARK WICKEN

Copyright © 2012 by The Mark Wicken Group

All rights reserved. No part of this book shall be reproduced, stored in a retrieval system, or transmitted by any means electronic, mechanical, photocopying, recording, or otherwise without permission in writing from the publisher. No patent liability is assumed with respect to the use of the information contained herein.

Launch Your Career
www.launchyourcareer.ca

First Printing: September 2012
ISBN: 978-0-9880500-0-6

Trademarks
All terms mentioned in this book that are known to be trademarks or service marks have been appropriately capitalized. The author cannot attest to the accuracy of this information. Use of a term in this book should not be regarded as affecting the validity of any trademark or service mark.

Warning and Disclaimer
Every effort has been made to make this book
as complete and as accurate as possible.
Every effort has been made to determine and acknowledge copyrights but in some cases copyright could not be traced.
The publisher offers apologies for any such omission and will reflect this in subsequent editions upon notification.
The author and the publisher shall have neither liability nor responsibility to any person or
entity with respect to any loss or damages
arising from the information contained in this book.

Cover design by Nicole Ellerton

Contact Mark Wicken
mark@launchyourcareer.ca

Dedication

To all the wonderful young people with
whom I've had the pleasure of teaching
throughout my career, who have inspired me
with their passion and enthusiasm,
and to my wife Nonie for her tolerance of
the hours I spent in front of my computer.
...Thank you.

Acknowledgements

A curtain call and standing ovation for all the players who have helped me on the voyage to complete this book and pursue my passion to help graduating students and first-time job seekers.

This book is the result of many meetings, conversations and emails with friends, colleagues and business professionals who have graciously given their time, guidance and counsel.

My appreciation and sincere thanks go to Harvey Botting, Robert McCulloch, Peter Brady, Bill Andersen, Michael Leuty, Jake McArthur, Nicole Ellerton, my sons Andrew and Chris, my wife Nonie, and every student I have had the pleasure of meeting and instructing.

A special thanks to Bob Lank who has helped me develop the strategies and thoughts you are about to read.

Foreword

Ever since I graduated from university and began my first job search (with a 10-page resumé that I thought captured all I WAS SURE people wanted to know about me), I knew at some level that there had to be a better way to approach the whole process.

My journey has taken me through Outplacement, Executive Search, Executive Transition, Change Management and Career Coaching. The common thread has been working with people going from something to something.

After several decades of working professionally with job seekers at many stages, I now know there are better ways and Mark has brought together a very practical collection of ideas, processes, and advice.

It has also been my pleasure to work with the Rotman School of Management for the last 11 years as a Mentor for a graduating MBA student. During these years, Mark and I have collaborated and presented to graduating MBA classes the whole topic of "Job Search - Myths and Realities." Many of these ideas are captured in this book.

I must get a request a week asking "Would you please look at my resumé and tell me what you think?" This would be like asking someone to read the middle chapter of a book and asking what did you think of the book! A resumé is just one part of a much bigger picture and must be aligned to what the job seeker is after. It is not where one starts!

The US Marines have a motto (loosely expressed) ..."Know thyself, know thy troop, and know thy mission." This is also a great starting point for a job seeker but it might be rephrased: "Know thyself, know how to communicate (about your skills/experience) and know what you want (your mission)."

What is ironic is that as you read Mark's book you may say to yourself, "I know there is nothing earth shattering here!" The fact is that there is often a WIDE gap in our lives between KNOWING and DOING; Common Knowledge versus Common Practice.

Mark offers us all an opportunity to learn new habits and what better time than when you are beginning your career journey. One underlying thought here is that everything matters during your search process. It is all about preparation and practice, just like an Olympic athlete; after all, it is a race!

When the race (your job search) actually starts, it's just part of the routine that he/she is already programmed to win. When he/she wins, it's just a natural extension of his/her preparation and routine - good habits kicking in. We are creatures of habit ... and I ask, what are yours like... every day?

If you are reading these words it means your journey has already begun. Congratulations! Have fun, learn lots and help others to do the same!

Of all the business books I have read on the topic of job search, no one has said it better or made it easier to understand and follow than Mark's book.

Bob Lank
Group Leader
CEO Global Network

Contents

INTRODUCTION..11

HOW TO USE THIS BOOK...12

CONGRATULATIONS!..14

CHAPTER 1   WHAT YOU NEED TO KNOW...................17

CHAPTER 2   THE HIRING PROCESS..........................23

CHAPTER 3   YOUR COVER LETTER..........................33

CHAPTER 4   YOUR RESUMÉ......................................47

CHAPTER 5   YOUR NETWORKING............................75

CHAPTER 6   YOUR JOB SEARCH.............................89

CHAPTER 7   YOUR INTERVIEW..............................109

CHAPTER 8   YOUR FOLLOW-UP.............................147

CHAPTER 9   NOW YOU HAVE THE JOB!................155

CHAPTER 10   YOUR TIME MANAGEMENT..............167

CHAPTER 11   SUMMARY..179

APPENDIX..185

MYTHS & REALITIES..209

BIBLIOGRAPHY...225

ABOUT MARK WICKEN..226

THE LAST WORDS..227

Introduction

You are reading this book because you have just graduated or you are starting your first job search. You are most likely full of excitement, anticipation and perhaps a little fear and anxiety. Don't worry, this is natural since you have never done this before.

I have written this book because I know your first job search is like no other you will ever have to do again and I found there is not much information specifically targeted to you, the first-time job seeker.

After 30 years of being involved in the hiring process, I've seen job search from all four perspectives…as a candidate going through my first job search, as an employer doing the hiring, as a recruiter connecting candidates with clients and as an educator teaching young people the fundamentals of looking for their first job. I understand job search from your position.

I've seen the mistakes and I have seen the brilliant techniques and behaviors that have led to "job-search successes."

This book mirrors the courses in job search I have taught over the years. I know the content is valuable and relevant to all graduates. Most of the book is common knowledge and I can assure you that everything is practical, easy to follow and effective. I have addressed the skills you need to be successful in your job search. These same skills will also serve you well throughout your career.

There are many things you can do to improve your chances of landing that first job. The most important thing you must do is to prepare for it properly and remain positive. I encourage you to follow this step-by-step process outlined in the book and apply it to your job search.

Good luck!

HOW TO USE THIS BOOK

Remember Me! is a step-by-step approach to job search for graduates and others who are entering the job market for the first time.

This book does not deal with your career choice. Hopefully the career service department at your school, college or university has given you guidance. There are many excellent web sites and books to help you with these decisions.

Most of you will have made a career choice while in school or at least made some decisions already about the type of job and industry you would like to pursue.

Although you may be tempted to jump to a chapter that is of immediate interest or concern, I suggest that you start from the beginning.

Follow each chapter so you can understand the "strategies" put forward in the book. Each chapter has a summary at the end and there are several worksheets in the Appendix to help you with the various disciplines of your search.

The book also contains certain points that are critical to your job search and I have highlighted them throughout as follows:

REMEMBER ME!
These are the points that will help create a lasting impression on everyone you will meet.

GREAT IDEA!
These are specific actions that will make you stand out and be remembered.

IMPORTANT!
These points are critical to your job search approach and things you need to understand to be successful.

DANGER!
These are the dangerous actions that could unknowingly jeopardize your job search. Avoid them.

Congratulations!

You have just graduated from school (University or College) or otherwise find yourself about to start your first "real" job search. You have never had to look for a job before. Summer jobs and part-time jobs may have come easily. Often you didn't even have to look for them…they came to you.

Now it is different. This is a unique time of your life and your career. It is the only time in your career that you will be leaving the academic world and entering the working world…the only time.

There are certain things you must know about your first job search that are different from most of the traditional information you will read.

Most people who are looking for a job have a history of experience that helps position themselves for the jobs they want to apply for.

You are right out of school and have no history beyond your part-time or summer employment. These jobs don't count from a practical experience standpoint, unless it is from an internship or co-op program. It is very unlikely you will be hired because of your part-time or summer job.

It is your education that has set your career path and what employers will be interested in. It is your behavior, personal characteristics and the way you present yourself during your job search that will set you apart from your competition.

In order to convince an employer you are the right person for the job, you must demonstrate behavior that shows you have the skills not only to do the job (which they know you have because of your education), but the skills necessary to succeed in your new business environment.

You represent willing potential. You represent the future of the industries and professions you have chosen to enter. In order to get hired you must convince the employer you are worthy of a chance to prove you are the right person and convince them that you *really* want the job.

This book will tell you how to do this by giving you the tools and strategies to be better than your competition. The job-search process is about the marketing and selling of "YOU." It is about building your image and presenting yourself.

This is your step-by-step coach to help land that first job. It will tell you how you can stand out from the competition and show potential employers you have the qualities they are looking for to meet their needs and the needs of the role.

This book cannot guarantee you will find a job, but it can guarantee you will be better prepared than the majority of people you will be competing against.

Read on...

Disclaimer

I make no excuses for the use of consistently overlapping key messages throughout this book. During my classes, workshops and seminars I often ask the group halfway through: "Do I repeat myself?"

Very sheepishly and often uncomfortably the response is always "yes." With that I know people are listening and getting the messages.

Throughout this book I will continually drive home the key points that are essential to your job-search success, so don't worry if you think you have read something before... you probably have and hopefully you will remember it.

"REPETITION IS THE
MOTHER OF LEARNING."
LATIN PROVERB

Chapter 1

WHAT YOU NEED TO KNOW

THIS MAY BE THE MOST USEFUL BOOK ON JOB SEARCH YOU WILL EVER READ AND THE ONLY ONE YOU WILL EVER NEED.

WHAT YOU NEED TO KNOW BEFORE YOU START

You have only one chance to make a first impression.

We form opinions about people the first time we see or meet them. "What you do," "What you say," "How you say it," "How you dress," or "How you eat your food," all create images and thoughts by which people judge you.

You CANNOT, *NOT* make a first impression when you first meet someone. Every contact after that first time either supports or conflicts with that first impression.

The job-search process has many parts and many people. As you enter the job market and start your job search you will be making first impressions every day. You will be meeting people for the first time and each person you meet could open the door to a job opportunity.

If you leave a good impression, that individual just might want to help you or think of you if he or she becomes aware of an appropriate opportunity.

Don't forget: nobody really knows who you are yet. The businesses and industries you want to enter do not know who you are. Your job is to make yourself known.

Think of yourself as a marketer. You are marketing a product and the product is YOU. Your brand is what people will think of you. As you go through your job search you will be creating that brand with everything you say and do. For this reason you want to make a great first impression with everyone you meet.

All Graduates Look The Same

Whether you like it or not, when you graduate from school, you and your fellow classmates will all look the same to the job market. You will all have your Diploma or Degree and you will all have your resumés.

Your success will depend on how you differentiate yourself from the competition and how you behave during your job search. This book will help you determine what to do, how to do it and why.

People who do the hiring hear the same things, every day, from every candidate. Your task is to get noticed, to differentiate yourself from all the other candidates and be remembered when the "decision to hire" is made.

The way you will do this is by executing all the steps in the hiring process, all the acts and behavior, better than your competition.

Why will this work for you? Simple! Most of your competition will make it easy for the hiring person to eliminate them from consideration by making simple mistakes. You want to be noticed and remembered for all the "right" reasons.

Often the difference between the person who gets the job and the one who doesn't is not academic preparation but how careful and strategic the graduate's job-search approach to potential employers is carried out.

The Secret To A Successful Job Search

- Know yourself plus the skills and attributes you possess

- Know the qualities all employers are looking for

- Understand the employer's hiring process better than your competition

- Be better informed than your competition about the companies you approach

That's all!

Chapter Summary

1 First impressions count. They really count in your job search. If you make a good first impression, you will be off to a great start. If it is poor, you might be out of the running before you begin.

2 All graduates basically look the same to the job market. You all represent "potential." Your job will be to give the employer a reason to hire *you*.

3 In a competitive market you need to use every job-search tool and technique you can to get that first job. Your success will be the results of the cumulative effort of all aspects of your search.

"SUCCESS IS NOTHING MORE
THAN A FEW SIMPLE DISCIPLINES
PRACTICED EVERY DAY."
JIM ROHN

Chapter 2

THE HIRING PROCESS

*IF YOU KNOW
WHAT THE EMPLOYER IS LOOKING FOR,
YOU CAN BE
WHAT THE EMPLOYER IS LOOKING FOR.*

Understanding The Hiring Process

You would like to believe that the hiring process is as simple as applying for the job, having an interview and receiving a job offer…and of course you would be wrong. In order to understand the hiring process, especially for students like you, right out of school, it helps to know how employers make decisions.

Most candidates make it easy for employers to make those decisions.

It is easier for an employer to find reasons NOT to hire someone rather than finding the reason to hire someone. Why? Because candidates make mistakes.

The incorrect name of the company or recipient on a cover letter, forgetting to sign the cover letter, an unprofessional-looking resumé, or worst of all, the dreaded "spelling mistake."

These errors will stop the employer cold. They will not read on. Their focus will shift to the next candidate. Why? They will conclude that if you cannot get important things right like your cover letter and resumé, you probably won't be able to get important things right on the job, if they hire you.

Competition and Choices

You will not be the only person applying for the job. There will be competition and there will be other equally qualified candidates working hard to get everything right. You must be better than the competition in everything you do.

The employer has choices. Since you are not the only candidate, if the employer finds reason to question your candidacy he/she will move on quickly to the next candidate and your chances are over.

Remember, this is a competition and the employer does have choices.

As in any competition, the person who wins is the person who trains the best and performs the best. It is the same in your job search.

A Race To The Finish

Have you ever been in a race?
Of course you have.
So, let's pretend you are in a race, a 100-meter dash and you are leading. As you approach the finish line you look over your right shoulder and see the person in second place is well behind you. You look over your left shoulder and the person in third place is even farther back. So, you *know* you are going to win and you just coast over the finish line.
The winner!

Now, let us pretend that looking for a job is like a race and crossing the finish line and winning means you get the job. As you move closer and closer to the finish you look over your right shoulder and you cannot see anyone. You look over the other shoulder...same thing. You do not know if you are in first, second or even third place. You might be tied for first. Are you going to let up? Are you going to coast the rest of the way? If you do, someone else might be trying just a little harder and "guess what?"

They might get there first.

In your job search you will not know if you are in first or second place in the race to get the job. If you really want the job you cannot let up, miss an opportunity to impress the employer or make one mistake.

One mistake or opportunity lost could be the difference between winning and losing. In the hiring process one person gets the job. Second and third place don't count.

Most of you will have the basic requirements for a typical entry-level job.

The best jobs do not go to the best qualified. They go to the best job seekers - the ones who execute the best job search and job-search strategies.

Common Knowledge And Common Practice

We are told and know we should say, "Please and Thank-you." Common knowledge, right? Is it common practice? Not always.

We are told and know we should send a "Thank-you" note after an interview. Common knowledge right? Is it common practice? Not always.

The difference between common knowledge and common practice in your behavior could be the difference between getting the job and not getting the job.

Remember, you have competition and the employer has choices. Hiring managers hear the same things every day from those applying for jobs. Be different, be noticed, be remembered.

You must differentiate yourself from the competition and stand out from the crowd to be successful.

The Moment Of Truth

In every hiring process there is a "moment of truth" when the hiring manager or decision maker must make a decision as to whom they should hire. After looking at all the cover letters and resumés, after all the phone conversations and interviews, they must decide.

"Who will I hire?" …This is the big question.

All candidates are qualified…often right out of school with their degrees or diplomas. No candidate has any practical experience. "Who will I hire?"

The answer is simple. They will hire the person they "Remember." The candidate they remember for all the right reasons…the candidate who said and did the things that were meaningful and important to the employer.

Therefore, in the hiring process, the most important thing you must keep in mind is that…"It is not about you."

This might sound strange, but it is not about you. The hiring process is about the person who makes the decision about the job that you want.

Your job is to help convince this person you are the right person for the job and that you want the job. Your job-search objective must be to get noticed and be remembered.

"REMEMBER ME!" Strategy

It is a fact: people *do* judge a book by it's cover.

People form opinions about others based on the signals or behavior conveyed. You might be the best and brightest, but if you present yourself poorly, especially with that first impression…unfortunately, that is the way you will be remembered.

Here is the key…

You must leave a positive **"Remember Me!"** impression with everyone you meet throughout your job search.

This must be your job-search strategy.

The reason is simple. If you leave a positive impression with everyone you meet, when opportunities arise and someone hears of a job position that is appropriate for you, they might remember you.

If people don't remember you, opportunities will be lost. If they do remember you for the right reasons, opportunities will happen.

When you approach a company you want to work for and a job you want, don't forget there will be others looking at that same job. They are your competition. When the hiring manager is ready to make the decision, you want to be the person they remember. Right?

You must find ways to create those **"Remember Me!"** impressions. You can create these impressions if you have a job-search strategy.

Hope is not a strategy. Luck is not a strategy.

"Remember Me!" IS a strategy.
"Remember Me!" is YOUR strategy.

A Word About Social Media... Google yourself.

It is undeniable that the Internet and social media have and will continue to have an impact on job search and the hiring process. Social media and your presence on it can work for you or work against you. Employers today almost always Google, check Facebook, LinkedIn and/or Twitter to see what they can find about the candidates they are considering to hire. If you use these social media to build your professional profile, it will no doubt help and work for you in your search. If your presence in social media has information or inappropriate content that reflect poorly on you, the employer will most likely dismiss you and move on to the next candidate. Remember, employers have choices. Build your profile on social media with your career goals in mind. Think about everything you post from the perspective of a potential employer.

Google yourself, a potential employer will.

Chapter Summary

1 Companies only want to hire people who will make a contribution to the success of their business. You must show them you can.

2 When applying for a job, you will have competition and the employer will have choices. Your job will be to convince them you are the "best" choice.

3 When all the interviews are over and the employer must make a decision who to hire, they will choose the person they remember for all the right reasons and behavior during the hiring process. You must create those reasons... those "Remember Me!" moments.

Chapter 3

YOUR COVER LETTER

A RESUMÉ WITH A "TO WHOM IT MAY CONCERN" COVER LETTER IS DESTINED FOR THE CIRCULAR FILE.

YOUR COVER LETTER

Your cover letter could be considered the most important written part of your job search and arguably the first impression an employer sees when you apply for a position.

Not sending a cover letter with your resumé is a big mistake.

Your cover letter tells the employer what you are applying for and why. It tailors your qualifications to that job. Clearly, the purpose of your cover letter is to get the reader's attention and persuade the employer to look at your resumé.

Bottom line...a good cover letter will help get your resumé read and help get you the interview.

Many people looking for a job will send their resumé without a cover letter. By sending a cover letter you could be differentiating yourself from many of your competitors.

Granted, some employers do not care about the cover letter while others might reject the resumé without one. You have no way of knowing how the employer feels, so send one anyway to be safe.

You will never be faulted for sending a great cover letter. What is the downside of sending a cover letter with your resumé? None!

Your cover letter must:

- Be customized to the company and directed to the right person

- Link your resumé to the opportunity you are applying for

- Qualify and clarify your reasons for sending your resumé

- Tell the reader why they should want to read your resumé

- Tell the reader why they should want to meet with you

- Focus on accomplishments rather than responsibilities

- Identify something *unique* about you that is relevant to the job

Your cover letter can:

- Create a great first impression

- Show you have done your research and show you know something about the company and industry

- Draw attention to your strengths and the most important facts on your resumé

- Address qualifications or criteria requested in a posted position

- Help the employer understand any gaps in your resumé or other points you feel need emphasis or clarification

- Show off your writing skills, your communication skills and your professionalism

- Express your enthusiasm for the job

- Tell the employer why you think you are suited for the job

- Set up the next step in the hiring process..."I will be calling you."

- Be an important **"Remember Me!"** factor

Using a cover letter template or using the same cover letter for every company you approach should be avoided and is a big mistake. You must customize your cover letter for each potential employer.

Remember...one spelling mistake and the employer stops reading.

Cover Letters

There are two types of cover letters.
Each one requires a different strategy.

> **1.** A letter responding to a specific *posted* position in print or on-line.

> **2.** A letter making a *"cold-call"* inquiry to see if there is an available position or opportunity.

1. Responding To A Posted Position

Posted positions indicate the hiring process will be formal and structured. A big part of how you will be evaluated in the hiring process will be how you respond to the posting.

Therefore you must:

- Follow all the instructions explicitly. You will be judged on how well you follow the instructions.

- Be sure your cover letter addresses the skills and experience appearing in the posted position…in fact, check them off!

- Repeat or use similar words used in the ad within your cover letter so they know you have carefully read the posting.

GREAT IDEA!
If you must send your cover letter and resumé by email, write the cover letter within the body of the email. Sending it as an attachment, it may not get opened first and may not even be read. Best of all, send the cover letter and resumé in the same document (cover letter first, of course).

Do not try to follow up after sending your letter. Usually the posted position will say that only those to be interviewed will be contacted. Trying to find out if they received your letter is a lame excuse to contact them and will only irritate the employer. You must wait for their reply.

2. Sending Your Cover Letter and Resumé, "Cold-Call."

Once you have done your research and identified the company you want to contact (see Chapter 6) you need to be very strategic in your approach.

- When sending your cover letter and resumé inquiring about the possibility of there being a position open, you must be specific and show you have knowledge of the company.

- Do your research on the company and type of job for which you are applying.

- Never send your cover letter and resumé "To whom it may concern."
  It will go nowhere... "No one is concerned."

- Address the letter to the right person, which means your research must determine who that person is. If your research cannot determine who that person is, send it to the most senior person you can identify in the department you are applying to. If that fails, send it to the President of the company. Yes, the President of the company. This will ensure it will get to the right person.

- Don't say at the end of your letter, "If you have any questions, please feel free to call and I will be happy to answer them." Simply say, "Please call if you have any questions or need more information."

- Always state at the end of the letter that you will be calling to follow up with that person.

- Mention any connections you might have at the company, especially if they have suggested you apply.

- Follow up right away or within the week for certain.

Make a "cold-call" a warm call by showing in the cover letter you have made an effort to know something about the company and the job.

Your "Cold-Call" Cover Letter Strategy

Sending a cover letter and resumé to a company "cold-call" can be a long shot. If you know they are hiring or if you know someone in that company, always include that information in your letter. What you are trying to do is to be there before they decide to post the position.

If this company is on your "most desirable companies to work for" list, you want to make sure you at least get the opportunity to meet with them. To do this, say in your letter that you would like to meet with them to discuss the possibility of employment.

If, when you contact them, they tell you there are no openings, you can ask for an informational interview to discuss possible opportunities in the future, within the industry or to get some advice on your job search. This approach may not always work but many people will give you some time if you approach them professionally and sincerely.

(I may get in trouble here with Human Resources Managers, but I suggest you never send your resumé to the Human Resources or Personnel Departments unless instructed to do so. The reason is simple. The Human Resources Department does not hire people. Part of their job is to keep unwanted or inappropriate resumés from cluttering the hiring person's "in file." They screen people and if there are no open positions at the company, all you will get is a nice "no thank-you" response back. If you approach the hiring person or the person who makes decisions you just might get an informational interview.)

GREAT IDEA!
Use a "Post-script" or PS after your signature to draw attention to something you really want them to know: *(PS: I have followed your web site and blog for the past several weeks and am very excited about the possibility of meeting with you)*...this shows you have done your research.
OR *(PS: I am certain my customer service experience will be of interest to you)... this shows confidence in your communication skills.*
Another **"Remember Me!"**

People read post-scripts.
They are powerful and get attention.

When Writing Your Cover Letter

- Remember, first impressions are lasting impressions and your cover letter *is* the first impression.

- Put "Private and Confidential" on the letter's envelope. Your personal resumé and information should be viewed only by the person you are sending it to.

- Get to the point at once, example: "Dear...I am writing to apply for the position of...which I saw advertised on..." (less is more.)

- Always make it clear to which position you are applying.

- State something about the job or industry that shows you have done your homework concerning the position.

- Highlight points on your resumé that show the qualities that you will bring to the position.

- Ask not what they can do for you, but tell them what you can do for them. Don't say what you *want*; say what you *offer*.

- Think "transferable skills" that are appropriate for the position.

- Emphasize any problem-solving experience, leadership qualities, and signs of entrepreneurial efforts in your past.

- State your desire to meet with them.

- Remember, you will be hired primarily for your accomplishments and the skills you have learned.

Your cover letter should convey:

**"This is why you should consider me."
...not "Look how interesting I am."**

Cover Letter Mistakes

Since your cover letter may be that first impression, it is imperative there are NO mistakes. Your cover letter must catch the reader's attention and want them to read on.

Fatal Mistakes:

- Addressing your cover letter, "To whom it may concern," or "Dear Personnel Manager."
  People hire people.
  (Always address your letter to a real person.)

- Telling the employer how they can help your career
  (Always tell what you can offer them.)

- Asking the employer to contact you
  (Always promise to call them.)

- Overusing the word "I."

- Repeating words in your resumé word for word in the cover letter

- Making your cover letter sound like a form letter

- Making your cover letter longer than one page

- Saying you will call and then not calling

- Forgetting to sign the letter

(SEE EXHIBITS 1 AND 2 FOR EXAMPLES OF COVER LETTERS)

(SEE EXHIBIT 3 FOR YOUR COVER LETTER CHECKLIST)

Name-Dropping Is Good!

It's not what you know, but who you know, what you know about who you know and beyond that, who knows you.

If you know someone who is currently working for the company you want to approach, don't be afraid to mention their name in your cover letter.

Companies like to know as much as they can about future employees, and if a trusted employee can endorse you it will work in your favor. Before you name-drop, there are a few guidelines.

- Speak with your contact to confirm they will actually be a referral.

- Ask if they know the hiring manager or the person to whom you should direct your letter and resumé. Ask what their relationship is. They may be able to give you some insight into the position or person.

- Make sure your contact is on good terms with the company and the hiring person.

- Give a copy of your cover letter and resumé to your contact before you send it to confirm that what you are saying about them is correct and appropriate.

- Always follow up with a "Thank-you" note to your contact after you have sent your resumé.

- Remember, this person is doing you a favor. Be respectful.

Chapter Summary

1. Always address your cover letter to a specific person. Never send or address your letter to the Human Resources department or "To whom it may concern," unless specifically instructed to do so.

2. Be certain your cover letter makes reference to the company, indicating you have done your research and are interested in the company.

3. Be sure to sign the letter and indicate you will await their call if you are applying a posted position. State you will follow up with a phone call, if you are applying "cold-call."

Chapter 4

YOUR RESUMÉ

YOU JUDGE YOURSELF
ON WHAT YOU KNOW YOU CAN DO.
WHEN HIRING, PEOPLE JUDGE YOU
ON WHAT YOU HAVE ACCOMPLISHED
AND MOST IMPORTANTLY,
ON WHAT YOU HAVE LEARNED.

Clarification...

Résumé Versus Curriculum Vitae or CV?

What is the difference? This is a question often asked by those entering the job market for the first time. For your purpose, there is no difference. People will use the terms interchangeably.

Technically, by definition, a résumé or resumé (either spelling) is a document used by individuals to present their background and skills...just what you will be doing.

A "Curriculum Vitae", often referred to as a CV, is a brief summary of one's career...which you are starting.

Since you are just starting your career, we will refer to this document throughout the book as your **"resumé."**

YOUR FIRST "REAL" RESUMÉ
In a world where a book is judged by it's cover...
What does yours say?

Employers have limited information on which to make decisions about whom they hire. Your resumé must help them make the right decision about you. Your resumé is not an exercise in self-validation. You are writing your resumé for someone else...not you. You are writing it for the decision maker, the person who will make the decision to hire you. Your resumé is your primary marketing tool and must reflect your job-search strategy.

You probably have a resumé. Your resumé might have been used to get a summer job or part-time work while you were in school. Things have changed and so have you.

If you are to land that first job, your resumé will play an important part of this process. You need to understand what it represents and what it is supposed to do. Even if someone offers to give you an interview without seeing your resumé, it is most likely they will say before the interview, "Send me your resumé."

What role does the resumé play in this process?

A resumé will not get you a job. It will get you an interview. This is the real reason you have a resumé. When someone reads your resumé it should answer one question and one question only:

"Do I want to meet this person?"

If the answer is "Yes," it has done its job and you now have a chance to impress a real person in a real-life situation: the interview.

Employers don't really care what *you* want. They only care about want *they* want. They are making an investment when they hire you. Will their investment pay off? This is the question they are trying to answer when they read your resumé.

What Is Your Resumé?

Most graduates would answer this question by saying it is a list of your past jobs and education. In fact it is much more than that.

You are the product and your resumé is the advertisement for that product. Your resumé is your marketing tool, an ad about you and your skills, telling the reader what you have to offer. The employer is buying your skills to put them to work; therefore, your resumé must tell the employer what you bring to the job.

If you ask 10 people for an opinion on your resumé you will undoubtedly get at least 10 different opinions. The only opinion that really matters is the opinion of the person who makes the decision about the job that you want. Your resumé must "target" that person, similar to advertising where an advertiser targets their message to a specific audience.

Your audience is that target and you want the response to the ad to be...

"I want to meet this person."

Your resumé could be that "first impression" referred to earlier. Granted, a cover letter accompanying your resumé might be the real "first impression." Your resumé in many cases may be the first thing the hiring person or manager sees. So what does your resumé represent?

- The most valuable piece of paper you own

- The first impression and the first thing the hiring person will see

- A summary of who you are and what you have accomplished

- An introduction to YOU

- An advertisement for YOU and an advertisement *about* YOU

You read an advertisement because it interests you and is targeted to you. It is the same with an potential employer.

Your resumé must be of interest and targeted to them. This means you must do your homework and write an effective resumé, targeted to the opportunity, the reader and the company.

All Graduates Look Alike

Everyone knows a resumé is biased in favor of the author. This is why most resumés look alike. To sell yourself and get the interview depends on standing out from the crowd, being noticed, and being remembered.

Your resumé must be intriguing enough to the reader to want to meet you while reaffirming that you can do and want to do the job.

Your resumé must be well organized, and easy to read and follow. It must be error free and must be tailored to the job to which you are applying. These key points will differentiate you from much of the competition. So...

Questions You Need To Ask Yourself

- **What is the purpose of the resumé?** To get the interview of course, but ask yourself: "Why would this company hire me?" and "What do I want them to know about me that will make me attractive to them?"

- **What should my resumé say about me?** You need to decide your key attributes, skills, interests, experiences and ambitions that would be meaningful to the reader.

- **What do I have to offer?** This is the question most students wrestle with. You offer "potential" …end of story. If you can show passion, energy and enthusiasm for the job, your chances of getting the job will be greatly increased.

Don't think you will be hired for your "new ideas and creativity." Remember, you likely haven't had any practical experience. Review the job description and identify the transferable skills you have that are applicable to what they are looking for.

- **What is relevant?** The employer is interested in skills you have learned that are transferable to the position you are applying for. Your schooling and part-time work have given you skills that will be of interest to them. Know what those skills are and be sure to state them in your resumé.

- **What quantifiable results can I show about my past?**
Determine memorable quantifiable things you have achieved or been recognized for and be sure to use them on your resumé.

> **When writing about results and accomplishments use the "So what?" test. Ask yourself... "What were the meaningful outcomes of those results?" and "How did it impact those around me?" Thinking this way will add substance and credibility to those achievements.**

- **Have I done my research?** Your resumé must be tailored to match the needs of the employer. So, before you send it out, ask yourself if you have done enough research on the job and company. Is this information reflected in your resumé?

- **Am I proud of my resumé?** If you are not happy with your resumé, do not send it to anyone until you are absolutely sure it is uniquely *yours*. Is it memorable?

Remember to include the results and accomplishments from your past and the skills you have learned.

"ACCOMPLISHMENTS ARE EVENTS IN YOUR LIFE THAT GAVE YOU A SENSE OF REAL SATISFACTION"
JIM HAYHURST SR.

The Best Format For A Graduate's Resumé

There are many different formats in resumé writing. Each format serves a different purpose. Some formats help explain career change. Some formats present a person with many different jobs in their background. These are usually called "Functional or Skill-Based" resumés.

As a graduate you will most likely not have a great deal of history to present, so the best format is a "Chronological Resumé."

A chronological resumé emphasizes dates of education and employment (full and part-time) listed in reverse chronological order, starting with the most recent information and working back in time.

(SEE EXHIBIT 4 FOR A SAMPLE RESUMÉ FORMAT)

Naming and Filing Your Resumé

Because you will most likely be sending your resumé by email at some point in your search, be sure to save your resumé in your computer with your full name as the "file" name. No abbreviations. Do not save it as "resumé.doc" and never send it as "resumé.doc" (Why? Most people do).

When an employer receives several resumés by email and all are labelled "your name"resumé.doc...Guess what they do with them? Don't expect an employer to re-name your resumé so they can keep track of it. They won't.

GREAT IDEA!
Put the name of the company to which you are applying after your name. Example: "Mark Wicken - Resumé - XYZ Foods"
Also: When sending your resumé by email, be sure to put your full name in the subject line. This will help the recipient find your resumé among the many others they receive. Another "Remember Me!"

Your Email Address

Have a professional email address...nothing cute, silly or nondescript. Make your email address your first and last name (plus a number if need be). The reasoning is simple. If someone is looking for your email in their in-coming mail and has trouble finding it because you didn't use your full name. It may get lost. Why take that chance?

If you want people to take you seriously about your career, have a serious email address..."rocketman@hotmail" may have been alright when you were in school but no potential employer is going to see the humor of this kind of language.

Do not use nicknames, hobbies, sports, sexual overtures or short forms in your email address. If you must keep your unprofessional personal email address, create a new professional address for your job search.

The best strategy? Use your full name.

Your Voice-mail

Your voice might be the first real "live" contact an employer has with you. Be sure the phone number you show on your resumé has a voice-mail and that you have an intelligent, professional, understandable voice message saying your name and "please leave a message."

A potential employer doesn't want to listen to your favorite music or your little sister or brother's greeting.

Consider a daily voice-mail message:

> *" This is Mark Wicken for Monday October 24th.*
> *I am not available to take your call.*
> *Please leave your name, number, and*
> *a brief message and I will return your call*
> *as soon as I am able.*
> *Thank you."*

Remember, your voice message could be that *first* impression.

What To Include On Your Resumé

The are hundreds of web sites with examples of resumés. The following are some simple rules to help you write the perfect chronological resumé. The order of the content is important because you are trying to create the picture of a person who will fit the reader's criteria. Most people scan resumés first, which means that the most important information needs to be up-front. The employer may not read your whole resumé.

Contact Information

- Include your name, phone numbers, and email addresses. Your address is optional. Only use a phone number if you have a voice-mail. Consider changing your message every day to be current with the date, letting the caller know when you will be returning the call.

- Include your LinkedIn address.
(Don't have one? Get one)

Career Objective

Always have an objective on your resumé. It is one of the first things the employer will look at and it should clearly state what you are looking for.

Your objective will most likely state you are looking for an entry-level position within the industry of your interested.

GREAT IDEA!
Customize the objective to the job description or title for which you are applying and include the name of the company. Use language like..."a position where I can use my skills and creativity to make a contribution to the success and growth of the company."

DO NOT under any circumstance use the words "to get experience" or "to learn." The reason is simple. An employer is not hiring you to give you experience. They will be hiring you so you can help them make their company better.
If you say you are looking for experience... what will you do once you get the experience? Leave that job for another job? That may not be what you mean, but it may be the way it is interpreted. Why take a chance?...don't use the words, "to get experience."

Profile (Optional)

A summary or profile is a section with an overview of what you have done and accomplished. It could also highlight those skills to which you want to draw attention.

Education and Training

This is the most important part of your resumé right now because, as a recent graduate, your education will be the most relevant part of the hiring criteria. This is why you are qualified for the jobs you are applying for.

- Include the name of your degree or diploma, the name of the institution, the location and the dates attended in reverse chronological order (most current first).

- You may choose to list some of the courses taken that are applicable to the job you are applying for.

- You may want to include your grade point average.

- You may want to include your high school if you have recently graduated or if some school activities or recognition are applicable to the position or company.

- If you only attended an institution for one or two years and did not graduate, put it down. It will be revealed eventually and should not (hopefully) be considered a negative if it helped you determine the career you really wanted to pursue.

Work Experience

- Include permanent, part-time positions, volunteer and other relevant experience. You may choose to use the heading: "Related Experience," if your experience is directly related to the position for which you are applying.

- Volunteer positions, co-op or field placements can also be listed under a separate heading.

- State your job title, dates of employment, name and location of the company.

    Qualify and quantify your experience and accomplishment and skills learned
    (Use the "So What?" test on page 53).

GREAT IDEA!
Describe each position using two sub-headings: "Responsibilities" and "Accomplishments *or* Skills Learned." The reasoning here is simple: if hired, you will be given responsibilities and expected to accomplish things.

The best indicator of future performance is past performance, so if you describe each position you have held in this manner, it will be easier for the reader to understand what to expect if they hire you.

The most important thing to remember when writing this part of your resumé is not to tell the reader "what you have done." Tell them, "what you have learned."

Just because you *say* you have done something does not mean you did it well or learned from it. If you focus on what you have learned, the employer can reasonably assume they won't have to teach you that skill or discipline.

Here are a few examples to describe experience in a meaningful way:

Weak... "Worked as a server in the hospitality industry where I served tables and greeted customers."

Versus

Stronger... "Worked as a server in the hospitality industry where I developed excellent customer service skills, teamwork and organization skills plus the ability to work under pressure and meet deadlines."

Weak... "Worked as a receptionist, answering phones, typing and filing."

Versus

Stronger... "Worked as a receptionist where I was the first point of contact for meeting and greeting all visitors, new clients and customers; thereby, developing strong communication and excellent interpersonal skills. I was the CEO of first impressions for my company."

Specialized Skills

- Highlight computer skills including hardware and software that might be applicable to the job you are applying for.

- Note language skills, oral and written as applicable.

- Highlight any special training, example: First-aid, CPR or other certifications.

- If your specialized skills are directly related to the position for which you are applying, you may choose to put the "Specialized Skills" section after your "Education" before your "Experience."

Awards and Special Accomplishments

- List all academic awards, special distinctions and noted honors. Always explain the award or distinction.

Interests and Activities

- List interests you have...hobbies, etc.

- Describe any volunteer work, etc.

This is the section in a resumé that many "so-called" experts will tell you is not relevant and is not required. They are wrong! What you like to do and your interests are a part of who you are. If you can show the reader you are an interesting person...*they just might want to meet you.* Depth of character is something employers look for.

References

- Do not include the names of references on resumé. Since you will be sending your resumé to many companies it is not appropriate to give the names and information about your references to everyone you contact. Only provide references, on a separate page, when they are requested. A reference notation such as "References Available Upon Request" is the best way.

If you are asked for three references, think about providing more if you can. This shows you are confident and have many people who will speak out for you.

Requesting References

When providing references it is best you use those people you have worked for or worked with who can speak about you in a work-related environment. Usually a potential employer will ask for three references.

Always approach a past employer or colleague to ask if they will be a reference for you. Always let them know when you have given their names to a potential employer so they can anticipate their call.

GREAT IDEA!
When someone agrees to be a reference for you, always send them a letter of thanks for their help and consideration. Also, send them your resumé and the job posting in advance. It is good manners and it is good business.
Another "Remember Me!"

Resumé Language Summary

Avoid using self-serving, self descriptions like "results oriented," "strategic thinker," "proven leadership"…boring! Use facts and examples to show your skills and qualities.

Tell people what you have learned, not just what you have done.
What you have learned, you will bring to the job.

Transferable Skills

Transferable skills are those skills you will have learned from school and part-time jobs. When you describe what you've done in your past jobs, instead of speaking about your non-related duties, speak about the skills you used when carrying out those duties.

Would an employer rather know that you served food in a restaurant or that you learned how to provide friendly and efficient customer service?

It is most likely your customer service skills will be of more importance. Here are a few more transferable skills for you to think about:

Communication Skills:

- Presented projects in school and developed presentation skills

- Wrote effective projects and correspondence

Think and Solve Problems:

- Researched and resolved customer issues and problems

- Read, analyzed and assessed information

- Developed critical thinking, ability to act logically and make decisions

Working With Others:

- Effectively worked as part of a team

- Developed leadership skills and an ability to motivate others

- Interacted with customers and clients

Organization and Management:

- Prioritized and handled multiple tasks simultaneously

- Managed an extensive work load at school

- Planned and organized all aspects of projects and events

- Ensured timely delivery of projects

Other Resumé Considerations

- Write in point form versus prose. Most people scan resumés and point form will stand out better.

- Put the most important information first.

- Use simple, clean fonts like Verdana, Arial, Trebuchet or Tahoma.

- Keep font size within the 9pt to 12pt range. Section or title headings can be a few points higher.

- Be sure all margins and indents are exactly correct. Sloppy formatting stands out and shows lack of attention to detail.

- Use a consistent format and alignment throughout.

- 1-2 pages maximum and number each page.

- Consider printing the second page on the reverse side (environmentally friendly).

- Do not shift tenses (use present and past tenses correctly).

- Put your name and contact information on every page.

- Use white paper. Fancy or colored paper could photocopy poorly.

- Use tones and graphics carefully and be sure they do not overpower the message.

Don't use every available highlighting format. There are several ways to highlight headings and sub-headings; bold face, capitals, italics or by using a different type face...pick ONE. Never use underlining except for URLs. The use of several different highlighting formats will make your resumé hard to read and look junky.

Quality Control Of Your Resumé

One mistake on your resumé could be the difference between getting the interview and not getting the interview. When employers find anything wrong with a resumé, *they stop reading*.

Here are some steps to follow so your resumé is error free.

- Take time to do it properly. Don't try writing your resumé in one day.

- Use spell-check, (then check it again because spell-check doesn't always work). Check grammar and punctuation.

- Always read your resumé out loud.

- Always have at least one other person read your resumé.

Read your resumé word for word…backwards. Do this at least one time. The mind sees what it wants to see. If you read your resumé backwards you will most likely find a mistake if there is one. How long will this take?…1-2 minutes? Is it worth it? One mistake and your chances of getting an interview are over. It is clearly well worth the 1-2 minutes to read your resumé backwards.

- Email your resumé to yourself and a friend to be absolutely sure there are no problems with it and to ensure clear transmission and receipt by employers.

You should have two versions of your resumé. One "hard copy" scannable copy to physically hand or mail to a perspective employer. One "digital" version that will email properly.

(SEE EXHIBIT 5 FOR YOUR RESUMÉ CHECKLIST)

Mistakes Graduates Make On Their Resumés

- **Unprofessional.**
  Using extreme or unconventional formats.
  Your resumé is your entrance to the job market. It must be professional and look like you are serious.

- **Carelessness.**
  Remember, one spelling mistake, bad grammar or punctuation, poor alignment...it is over!
  Employers will judge the quality of your future work by the quality of the resumé (and cover letter) you present to them.

- **Misrepresentation.**
  Embellishing the truth, telling untruths, distorting facts...any misrepresentation will come back to haunt you.

- **Overkill.**
  Exaggerating your responsibilities or accomplishments.

- **Excessive Language.**
  Overuse of superlatives or subjective language.

- **Being underwhelming.**
  You get one chance to leave a first impression. Be impressive. State what you are good at and what you are proud of.

- **Vague language.**
  Using unconventional or ordinary language like "I have good communication skills", "I get along well with people"...What does this mean? Out of context, without specifics or examples these types of comments are meaningless. Be explicit.

- **Unsupportive claims.**
  Making claims on your resumé that you cannot back up with examples.

- **Long-winded sentences.**
  Lengthy sentences can get boring. Keep language simple and sentences short.

- **Cuteness or over personalizing.**
  No gimmicks. Unless your creative idea is brilliant, don't take a chance. No smiley faces or meaningless graphics.

- **Resumé "Speak."**
  Avoid resumé and business cliches..."Taking something to the next level," "Thinking outside of the box." Nobody really knows what these words or phrases mean, so stay away from trendy language.

- **Distinctiveness.**
  Your resumé will stand out from the others if you avoid these mistakes.

REMEMBER...Anything that can be misunderstood *will* be misunderstood, reducing your chances of getting an interview. Remember that when someone is reading your resumé you are not there to defend or explain it.

**A "winning resumé"
is the one that
gets you the interview.**

Chapter Summary

1. Your resumé "Objective" should always be customized to the job to which you are applying, avoiding words like: "...looking to get experience."

2. Describe what you have learned, not what you have done. What you have learned, successes and accomplishments are what the employer is interested in.

3. Before you send your resumé anywhere, use spell-check. Then recheck the spelling, grammar and punctuation. Read your resumé out loud, then read it backwards and have someone else read it. Done this?
OK, now you can send it.

Chapter 5

YOUR NETWORKING

*YOU DON'T NEED TO KNOW
THE MOST PEOPLE.
YOU JUST NEED TO KNOW
THE RIGHT PEOPLE.*

NETWORKING

"It's not *what* you know that counts, it's *who* you know and what you know about who you know."

We have heard this many times. It is true.....but what is even more important is... **"Who knows you?"**

When you leave school, with the exception of your immediate circle of friends and relatives, no one really knows who you are. No one in the industry you want to enter knows who you are...so, how do we fix this?

We have all heard the term networking and most of us have a pretty good idea what it is about. What you need to know is that this will be the most important business and job-search tool you will ever need.

Do you have one? Of course you do. Everyone has a network of people that includes friends, family and acquaintances, some close, some remote and you do have them. Most of us don't think of our network when we start our job search because we don't think our friends know anything about the jobs we are looking for. This would be your first mistake.

You may have heard the common term: "Six Degrees of Separation" (also referred to as the "Human Web"). It refers to the idea that everyone is, on average approximately six steps away from any other person on earth. A chain of "a friend of a friend" statements can be made, on average, to connect any two people in six steps or fewer.

We are all connected to each other. You know someone, who knows someone, who knows someone, etc. If you do the math it makes sense. The people you want to know, the people you want to approach in your job search are probably within your reach through your network. You just have to find them.

Most of the successes in your life will be the result of cooperation and help of others. If you don't develop a good network of "relationships" you may never know how successful you could become. You do not have to do it all yourself if you have a network of friends and associates to draw on.

What Is Networking?

Networking is the process of developing and nurturing relationships. It can be the single most effective method of gathering career-related information and developing contacts. Most importantly networking is the best way to uncover the hidden job market. It will no doubt contribute to your overall business success.

Your Network

Your network will become an organized collection of your personal and professional contacts which in turn opens up your contacts' networks. It is a two-way street and is a lifetime quest - not just for job hunting.

What Can Your Network Do?

- It can help you get started in your job search
- It can help you help others
- It can help uncover jobs not advertised
- It can help you get inside knowledge of companies and their needs
- It can help you learn the names of decision-makers and influential people
- It can provide new directions and experiences
- It can provide job security
- It can make you look good in front of your boss and peers
- It can save you (and your company) time and money

How Do You Prepare And Build Your Network?

- Make a list of everyone you know
- What do you know about them?
- Who do they know?
- Start a data base…you just started your network

Everyone you know is part of your network.

Networking is consistently cited and the number one way for graduates to get their first job. Remember, most of the jobs available never get advertised. They are the "hidden" job market.

Your "Elevator Speech"
(Your Verbal Business Card)

You will meet many new people in your job search. What will you say?

One of the most important skills a job seeker can have is to be able to sum up their situation in a few short minutes. There will be many times in your job search, either networking or an unexpected introduction, when someone will say: "Tell me about yourself" or "What do you plan to do when you graduate?" It will be important to clearly and succinctly tell them who you are and what you are doing.

This short speech is often called "The Elevator Pitch" - so named because it should last no longer than the average elevator ride and reflects the idea that it should be possible to tell someone about yourself in the time span of an elevator ride, or approximately 30 seconds to two minutes. You meet someone you have always wanted to work for and you have 30 seconds. What will you say?

Being prepared to deliver your elevator pitch will ensure you will always be able to take advantage of situations when there are people you want to network with or people who might provide you with a job lead or introduction.

The first goal of any meeting or conversation is often to have a second one, so when you meet someone in a networking environment your object should be to connect and follow up with another meeting or conversation in a more suitable, controlled environment where you can present yourself completely.

These types of encounters will usually be first impressions, so you want to appear articulate, professional and confident.

Preparation is the key to confidence. Here are a few tips:

- Write out your speech and always have it ready.

- Be specific. Know what you want people to remember about you.

- Let people know what your goal is and what you want.

- Keep it short. People have a limited attention span.

- The more you practice, the better you will be.

- Let your enthusiasm and passion show.

- Show interest in the person you are addressing. Remember, it is just as important to listen as it is to talk.

> "BE CLEAR. BE BRIEF. BE SEATED."
> WINSTON CHURCHILL

Sample Elevator Speech…

"Good afternoon, Mr. Smith. Nice to meet you. My name is Mark Wicken and I have just graduated from XYZ University and am currently looking to start my career in advertising. I understand you work for ABC Agency. Could you tell me how you started your career in advertising?"

**Prepare your "Elevator Speech" and be ready to deliver it anytime, anywhere. It could change your life and open new doors.
Another "Remember Me!"**

Effective Networking Behaviors For Graduates
Most job openings are never advertised.

Networking events or any business gatherings offer excellent opportunities to introduce yourself to a select, targeted group of people. These people are potential sources of referrals.

How you introduce yourself will make an impact on them and will determine whether or not they actually remember you.

Networking is a marketing and business tool. It is an art to know how to network effectively. Here are ideas on making the most out of networking opportunities.

- **Join the right groups.** Look for those organizations, clubs, and events, whose members have interests and activities similar to yours.

- **Plan your approach in advance.** Don't go to a networking function unprepared. Know in advance who will be there, and the agenda.

- **Get organized.** Bring something to write with and on. You may need to write down a name or address, or make a note to yourself.
Today's handhelds and tablets make it convenient and the information can later be downloaded to your computer.

- **Arrive early.** If there is a list of attendees or participants, read it.

- **Have a business card.** Even if you are still a student or graduate, have a business card with your contact information. You want to be able to give the right people your card as a reminder so you can follow up afterwards and so they will remember you.

- **Develop a conversation.** Have your introductory "elevator speech" ready and rehearsed so when you meet someone you can deliver it and open the dialogue. A networking function is an ideal way to have people get to know you.

- **Seek out the right contacts.** Don't wait for people to come to you. If there is someone at the event with whom you want to become acquainted, seek them out.
- **Debrief.** Check your notes after the networking event to remind yourself of a person or specific conversation.

- **Follow Up Right Away.** Do not waste time. Follow up with a phone call, note or email as soon as possible to re-connect and keep the dialogue open.

- **Keep Records.** Keep track of all the people you meet and their interest. Always remember to thank them for input and referrals.

One of the most common questions graduates have about meeting people for the first time or at networking events is "What do I say?" The easiest way to start a conversation is to ask a question.

When you first meet someone you do not have to begin by talking about yourself. Simply ask them about themselves...ask: "How did you get started in the business?" or "How did you start your career?" People like it when you are interested in them.

Keep in mind that the number one topic of conversation most people like talking about is themselves.

When you meet someone for the first time be sure to listen for their name, offer a firm handshake, make eye contact and be sure to smile. The secret to being a good networker is being a good listener.

"LISTENING IS NOT A SKILL,
IT IS A DISCIPLINE.
ALL YOU HAVE TO DO
IS KEEP YOUR MOUTH SHUT."

PETER DRUCKER

Reasons To Stay In Touch With Your Network

The first step you should take at the beginning of your job search is to contact your network of friends, colleagues, family and acquaintances to let them know of your availability and your search goals. There are many reasons why it is important to continually call or write people in your network to stay connected. Here are some good reasons to do so:

- You may need them when you are looking for a job
- You may want feedback on your resumé
- You may want to ask them to be a reference
- You may want them to be referrals
- You may want advice on work or a job-search issue
- You may want them to tell you about jobs as they become available in their company

Networking is a long-term investment in your future. Start building your network now and it will stay with you forever.

"THE SINGLE CHARACTERISTIC SHARED BY ALL TRULY SUCCESSFUL PEOPLE IS THEIR ABILITY TO CREATE AND NURTURE A NETWORK OF CONTACTS."

HARVEY MACKAY

Keeping Your Network Current and Active

Statistically, the most effective resource for finding a job is networking. Networking is a business behavior you will use your whole career. Your network is yours forever if you treat it properly and with respect. Follow these rules and your network will always be there when you need it.

- Find reasons to keep in touch with people
- Don't wait until you need someone before you contact them
- Contact people regularly (once a year at least)
- Send personal messages, not mass emails or letters
- Remember personal information (birthdays, promotions, etc.)
- Initiate conversation with people as often as you can
- You do not have to make friends with everyone, but you can keep in contact with everyone in your network
- Avoid burning bridges by maintaining good relationships. Make everyone in your network your ally
- Look for reasons to reach out to your network as often as you can

Relationships take time and networking is about systematically and patiently cultivating business relationships. You seldom see immediate results. It takes time for relationships to grow.

There are many Internet networking sites. Facebook is perhaps your social network. Do not confuse your social network with your business network and be careful what you post on your social site because it could find its way into your business world.

LinkedIn

LinkedIn is an excellent business networking site. Start a profile, have a LinkedIn address, put it on your resumé and make it part of your job search and career development.

Remember, employers check the Internet and often the first thing they do when they receive a resumé is to Google the person.

Make the Internet and your presence on it work for you not against you. The Internet is another marketing tool for your job search.

Chapter Summary

1 — Networking is a skill and one of the most important disciplines for business success. It will be the most important tool in your job search.

2 — Always be prepared to deliver your "elevator speech." You never know when the perfect opportunity to use it will occur.

3 — Keep in touch with your network on a regular basis. Remember, it is not who you know but who knows you and how they remember you that carries forward into your future.

> "THE REASON THAT THE
> PEOPLE-TALKING-TO-PEOPLE
> TECHNIQUE WORKS SO WELL
> (IN JOB SEARCH)
> IS THAT PEOPLE HIRE PEOPLE."
> ORVILLE PIERSON

Chapter 6

YOUR JOB SEARCH

"THERE ARE NO SECRETS TO SUCCESS. IT IS THE RESULT OF PREPARATION, HARD WORK, AND LEARNING FROM FAILURE."
COLIN POWELL

YOUR JOB SEARCH

Employers want to hire people who will make their businesses successful.

For every graduating student looking for a job, there is an individual...one person...in the industry who will ultimately make the decision to hire you.

The task in your job search is to identify that person and do everything you can to convince him/her "you" are the right person for the job. Sounds simple? It can be if you take the right approach and do the right things.

The best approach will be to prove you are the right match for the position by conveying your education, experience and accomplishments in a clear concise manner and by demonstrating your knowledge of the position, company and industry.

The two biggest mistakes graduates make are not being able to articulate what they can bring to the position and not knowing enough about the job and/or the company to which they are applying. Both can be deal breakers.

Once you have determined the job you want and/or the industry you want to enter, your "job-search strategy" will be critical to your success.

By definition:
> **Your "Objective" defines what you want to do.**
> **Your "Strategy" defines how you will do it.**

Job Search Approaches

There are many ways to look for a job. Some are obvious and some not so obvious. There is no right or wrong. Whichever one works is the right one. There are limitations to some approaches, so you want to maximize your opportunities by being strategic and not relying on only one or two.

Is job search a science or an art? The answer is both. The way you go about your job search with research, objectives, strategies, target companies etc. is the science. Anyone can do it. The "art" in job search is doing it creatively using all the tools you have at your disposal - cover letter, resumé, interview, etc., in unique ways that make you stand out from the competition to be noticed. Most importantly…to be Remembered.

School and Career Services Departments. Your school most likely has a great career services department with people whose job it is to promote the school and help you with your search. Do not ignore them. Listen to them and use their advice. You paid for it and they know what they are doing. It is important not to rely on school as your only source of job leads.

Mailing out resumés to HR Departments. A letter and resumé sent to the Human Resources department of a company with no specific position targeted is probably a waste of time. It will most likely get thrown away or perhaps filed. Remember, HR departments do not usually hire people, they screen candidates. They are not the decision makers.

Responding to Newspaper Ads. If you apply to positions posted in newspapers, you will probably be one of hundreds who will respond. It will be difficult, if not impossible, to stand out.

Search Firms and Placement Services. Search firms work for a client, not you. If you use a search firm, you have a price on your head because the firm will charge the client a fee for their service. Rarely, if ever, would a company use a search firm to find an entry-level candidate.

The Internet and Job Boards. Technology is wonderful and there are hundreds of job boards for every industry and occupation. And, yes, once a job is posted, there are hundreds, if not thousands, of respondents.
How do you stand out? How do you get noticed?
The answer is *you don't* and *you can't*. With the Internet, you are sending your resumé to a person or company and it is almost impossible to follow up. While there is always a chance you might get selected, in all likelihood you will never hear back. The Internet is a great research tool. It will not make you smart. Used properly, the Internet will make you smarter in your job search.

Cold Calling. Pure cold calling is a very dangerous way to approach a company. It is like being an uninvited guest. If you just show up at a company's front door asking to see someone about a job and the person you approach is busy, your "first impression" could work against you.
A cold call is like rolling the dice and hoping luck is with you. Remember, luck is not a good job-search strategy.

Self-Marketing Approach. The highest success rate in the job-search market is by building and using your network. All the statistics show the majority of successful job searches are the result of referrals and networking. The reasoning here is simple: People trust those they know. If you are referred or connected to a potential employer by someone the employer knows, your chances of getting an interview are greatly increased.

This should be your job-search strategy.

The Hidden Job Market. Most graduates spend their time look for "job postings" instead of trying to reach the decision maker before there is a job opening or a position posted. Published job postings represent perhaps 15%-20% of the available jobs in a marketplace. This varies from market to market, but your best opportunity of finding a job will be in the "silent or hidden job market."
The ones you find on your own through your network. The jobs that are not advertised.

Create "Remember Me!" moments with everyone you meet in your job search. If you do this properly, referrals and introductions will follow.

Your Job-Search Strategy

Job-search success is not about academic preparation, but a fine-tuned, customized approach to a specific employer. This section of **"Remember Me!"** might be the most important part of this whole process. Clearly, if you do not get an interview, you will not get a job. So just getting in the door will be the toughest part.

Once you have identified the company or companies you want to work for, the process has started. You can never have too much knowledge about the company and the job. This will be valuable when you get to the interview stage.

First, you must understand that your first job search is the beginning of your career, and is unlike any other situation in your life. You are right out of school, eager to start and passionate about the career path you have chosen. Employers need to know this and will never fault you for being persistent in your pursuit of that first job.

As long as you are professional, polite and personable you will never be faulted for being enthusiastic.

Every person currently working in the industry you want to be in, at some point did not work in the industry. We all have to start somewhere.

You have just graduated and are determined to get started. If you present yourself professionally, most people you approach will likely be courteous and considerate. Why? Because they just might remember when they were in your shoes. You need to keep this in mind and play this card as often as you can. Here is how.

Your Job-Search Approach

We have discussed the difference between responding to a posted position and the "self-marketing" approach on cover letters in Chapter 3. With your "self-marketing" approach once you have done your networking, your research, prepared your resumé, and made your "hit-list" of those people and companies you want to approach. You are ready to begin.

Since you cannot be absolutely sure the companies you are approaching have a position open, your strategy should be to get face-time with the right people and and a chance to introduce yourself to them. This will set you up for possible future consideration and, more importantly, it will start to build your network.

Here are the steps to follow:

- First, you are going to send your cover letter and resumé as a hard-copy, not email. Avoid email being the first impression at all costs. Why? Because you will look just like everyone else who approaches that company by email. There is always the risk that the formatting of your cover letter and resumé gets altered in the transmission, which means your first impression will be negative.

- Direct your customized cover letter and resumé package to a specific person at the company. For this example we will say we are sending it to the President, Mr./Ms. Smith.

- Send your resumé package by courier or priority post mail. When it arrives, it will go directly to Mr./Ms. Smith and not the mail-room or human resources. In your cover letter remember to say you will be calling him/her to follow up.

- Your package will arrive within a day or two, which means you are ready to follow up with a phone call to Mr./Ms. Smith.

- You are going to call Mr./Ms. Smith, BUT you do not actually want to speak to him/her. You are going to leave a message, a voice-mail. How do you do this? Quite simple. You call after hours. (You can always get a person's voice-mail after hours by going through their directory or calling during the day to get the extension). Remember you do not want to speak with him/her at this point.

- Why do you not want to speak with Mr./Ms. Smith? Let's say you call and actually speak to Mr./Ms Smith, and he/she has not yet received your cover letter and resumé. Would this be an awkward conversation?...a poor first impression? Of course.

This is why you are calling ahead with a message that says:

"Mr./Ms. Smith, my name is Mark Wicken and I am calling to confirm that you have received my cover letter and resumé. I have just graduated from XYZ School and am very excited about starting my career and was hoping I might meet with you to discuss possible opportunities with your company. I will call you tomorrow to see if there is an appropriate time for us to speak or meet. I look forward to speaking with you. Thank you."

- Your phone script is very important because you want to leave a good first impression. So write out your script and rehearse it before you call. If you call after hours and actually *do* speak with Mr./Ms. Smith directly…you will be ready.

Now, several things might happen as a result of the message you leave:

- If Mr./Ms. Smith has seen your package, he/she might call you back.

- If Mr./Ms. Smith has seen your package, he/she might await your *next* call.

- If Mr./Ms. Smith has *not* seen your package, they might look for it knowing you are going to call back.

- Mr./Ms. Smith might have someone else call you back to follow up to set up a meeting or simply to say "no thanks."

No matter what happens, from your voice-mail message Mr./Ms. Smith knows who you are and what you want.

He/she knows you are confident, pleasant, friendly and that you have good communication skills.

A good first impression? Certainly!

Remember, Mr./Ms. Smith has not met you yet and he/she is already drawing some conclusions about you.

- Next, you will call Mr./Ms. Smith as you said you would. This time you *do* want to speak directly with him/her. The best times to call are between 8:00 and 9:00 a.m. before people start to work or after 5:00 p.m. at the end of the day.

Remember, people work 9 to 5 and you don't want to be an interruption. It may take several times to get hold of Mr./Ms. Smith. It is appropriate to now leave your number for a call back (making sure that you will be there to take the call). You might identify the best that time you would be available to take a call back.

You could also say when you plan to call back or you could ask for them to let you know if there is an appropriate time for you to call back. All the time you are saying YOU will do the calling back, not inconveniencing Mr./Ms. Smith by asking them to call you unless they choose to do so.

GREAT IDEA!
If when trying to reach Mr./Ms. Smith you get the receptionist or assistant and they might say: "Who is calling?"…you can honestly say: "This is Mark Wicken. May I speak to Mr./Ms. Smith…he/she is expecting my call." Do not say you have sent your resumé or you are looking for a job because if you do you might get shipped off to personnel or human resources.

Let's say you finally speak to Mr./Ms. Smith directly. Have your script ready with your story and ask for an interview. There are several scenarios that could evolve here. Let discuss the possibilities.

- Mr./Ms. Smith might agree and set up a time for an interview. Perfect!

- Mr./Ms. Smith might say they are not hiring and there are no openings. If so, you request the opportunity to meet with him/her to get some advice and direction on your career.

- Mr./Ms. Smith says no!
  If so, you ask if there is anyone else in his/her company that you could speak with to get some advice and direction on your career.

- Mr./Ms. Smith says no!
  If so, you ask if he/she knows of any other companies that you might approach because you have just graduating and are just starting your career and would appreciate some help.

- Mr./Ms. Smith says no!
  If so, you can ask if it would be alright for you to call back in a month or two to see if the situation has changed.

- Mr./Ms. Smith says no!

Realistically what do you think the chances are that Mr./Ms. Smith will say "No" to all these requests? If you are professional and polite you will get something valuable out of the conversation.

If Mr./Ms. Smith does say "No" to all your requests, you have probably identified a very unfriendly, miserable individual you wouldn't want to work with anyway.

GREAT IDEA!
Always be ready to leave a voice mail when you call someone. When you call during business hours, you will often get voice-mail.
Anticipating this, always have your script in front of you when you call. Leave a clear, professional, succinct message.

Be Persistent But Be Patient:

Don't blame the employer. When trying to reach someone by phone, don't be surprised if it takes several attempts before you reach them. Being persistent is much better than being out of work. You will not be faulted for persistence. If someone really wants you to stop calling...all they have to do is tell you to stop calling.

Tips For Conducting Your First Job Search

- **Treat your job search as a business.** You are a sales executive for your business selling a product and the product is **you**.

- **Networking starts at home.** Ask your parents and friends for business contacts.

- **Get your foot in the door.** Use part-time jobs or internships to get in the door so you can prove what you can do.

- **Use school ties.** Teachers with contacts in your field of interest can help open doors. Use them.

- **Venture out.** Be visible. People hire people, not names or resumés. Attend events in the field of interest you want to be in. Network. Network. Network.

- **Use the Internet effectively.** Learn to use Internet tools for research, not contact. Whenever possible, make face-to-face contact with the companies you want to work for.

- **Plan a daily schedule.** Have specific hours during the day that you are at your desk working to find a new job. Be sure to leave time for exercise and friends.

- **Set aside enough time to do the job search well.** Be realistic about the time you need to do these tasks. If you do not allot enough time, you will be careless about the job applications.

- **Keep meticulous records.** Keep track of the jobs you have applied for:…when, where, and with whom you have had interviews and conversations. Following up will be easier if you have the information all in one place. Keep notes on phone conversations and interviews.

- **Check your voice-mail and email regularly.** You do not want to miss a call, or delay in responding to people trying to reach you. It could be a lead, or even better, a call to set up an interview.

- **Have other meaningful work.** Do some volunteer work or contract work. It gives you something to talk about when you interview and makes you feel productive and useful. Volunteer work is a great way to network.

- **Stay positive.** Do what it takes to keep happy and optimistic. No one wants to hire someone who is angry or sad.

- **Find a partner or coach to help**. A job search can be isolating. Find a friend or a coach to talk with regularly. Tell him/her what is happening in your search. Brainstorm and strategize with your friend or coach. Rehearse with the person when you have an interview or when you are going to make an important call.

- **Work to objectives.** Set realistic goals that you are able to accomplish...number of networking contacts, number of interviews etc.

- **Track your progress.** Know every stage of your job search and evaluate your successes and difficulties.

- **Strengthen your confidence.** Do whatever it takes to make you feel confident and happy during your job search. This may mean part-time work or being with people who recognize you as the capable person you are. You must always exude confidence and energy.

Remember, everything you are doing is designed to create and build your "Remember Me!" moments.

(SEE EXHIBIT 6 FOR YOUR JOB SEARCH WORKSHEET)

Mistakes To Avoid When Contacting An Employer

- **Submitting your cover letter and resumé using every format.** Don't email and hardcopy. One submission is sufficient.

- **"Stalking" the employer.** Calling and emailing daily to follow up looks needy and will not encourage the employer to contact you.

- **Failing to call.** If you say in your cover letter you will call…call.

- **Ignoring the employer's direction.** If you disregard directions in the submission of your qualifications, do not expect a response.

- **Calling the employer to ask for more information about the job.** If you see a position advertised that looks appealing, just go for it.

- **Forgetting to include your resumé attachment with your email.** (no one has ever done this before!)

- **Asking if the job is still open within a week or two of a posting**. Whether the job is open or not is irrelevant. You want to give yourself as many options as possible to get your resumé on file, especially if the employer's initial offer isn't accepted or an additional candidate is needed.

- **Expecting the employer to do your homework.** It's your job to research the employer. Search the Internet, go to the library, and utilize your network to get information about the company.

- **Sending a resumé without a cover letter.** Simply stated, most employers view this as being lazy.

- **Making it hard for the employer to figure out what you are applying for**. Employers frequently have more than one opportunity available; thus it is important that you always specify the position for which you are applying.

Guidelines To Using Email Effectively

Email is now a common means of communication. People understand the importance of making a good impression in face-to-face meetings, but then don't take the effort to make a good email impression.

If you want to make a good impression, here are a few tips:

- **Have a professional email address.**
  Upgrade your address from dude@abc.com, to a professional address like, j.smith@abc.com.

- **Email contact details.**
  Have standardized email contact details with all your information.

- **Check incoming mail regularly.**
  Once a day is not enough.

- **Respond to each message immediately.**
  At least within 24 hours.

- **Write in complete sentences with no missspelling.** *(oops!)*

- **Answer all questions.**
  If the message to you has questions, make sure to answer them completely.

- **Longer is better.**
  Explain yourself completely. Misunderstandings can happen easily.

- **Don't send a message all in caps.**
  It looks like you are **SHOUTING!**

- **Verify that your attachments are being received.**
  Sometimes there is a mismatch between your encoding format and the recipient's decoding format and the recipient cannot read your attached file. Save and send your documents as PDFs so they can be read correctly.

- **Use the phone periodically.**
  It is more personal than using email.

- **Consider entering the recipient's address last.**
  Compose your email, enter the subject, add the attachments and then put in the recipient's address. This could avoid accidentally sending the email before it is completed or before you have added the attachments.

- **Etiquette requires some communications to be written and mailed.**
  Use good judgment when sending confidential information.

Chapter Summary

1. Job-search success will depend on how well you conduct your search. Organization, research and networking will be the keys to your success.

2. Focus your efforts on the "self-marketing" approach where you are in control. Don't rely on job postings or people finding you. The more people you meet and contact, the better your chances of success.

3. Your job search is the beginning of your career. Everyone you meet and every company you approach could be a part of your future. Research, hard work, preparation, and persistence will pay off.

Chapter 7

YOUR INTERVIEW

*YOU ONLY GET ONE CHANCE
TO MAKE THAT FIRST IMPRESSION
...MAKE IT COUNT.*

YOUR INTERVIEW

**Your resumé will get you the interview,
but it is the interview that will get you the job.**

The next stage of your job search has started. Up to now it has only been your resumé telling people who you are. Now you have an interview. Everything has changed. Your resumé got you the interview and now it is up to you.

It is very important that you do everything you can to convince the employer you are the right person for the job. Your behavior throughout the interviewing process will be critical to their final decision.

You may be the brightest, most qualified person, but if you cannot present yourself in a professional, confident manner, the employer will never know. Remember, there is competition and the employer will have choices.

Your interview will likely be the first "in person" contact you will have with the potential employer.

**First impressions are critical.
You must be prepared right from the beginning.**

Clearly, an interview is a "staged event." The interviewer knows the questions they are going to ask. You will come prepared to present yourself as well as you can. In reality, the interviewer will never know if you are the right candidate until they actually put you to work. Everything you will have done at school has prepared you for this, but until you actually start working, no one will know how you will perform.

For this reason, your interview will be critical in the decision-making process. Your behavior, pre and post interview, your personality and the way you answer the interview questions will all be indicators of future behavior. This is how you will be evaluated.

What Employers Look For In An Entry-Level Employee

Employers are looking for the personality traits that will help them determine if you are a good candidate and a good hiring risk. More importantly, they will be trying to determine if you will fit into their work environment and get along with their employees...the people you will work with.

Professionalism is something you will need to prove to employers the very first time you have contact with them.

The qualities of being professional are simple: confidence, dependability, enthusiasm, flexibility, strong work ethic. These qualities are what every employer is looking for.

How does the employer determine if you really have these qualities? Not from your resumé. They can only uncover these qualities through the interviewing process.

It is up to you to present yourself that demonstrates and reinforces these qualities.

Interviewers are influenced by many things, but there are four main areas or criteria that will influence the employer most during the interview.

They are:

- ✓ **Job qualifications**

- ✓ **Image and appearance**

- ✓ **Communication skills**

- ✓ **Attitude, motivation, energy, passion and enthusiasm**

By the time you get to the interview stage of your job search you will have already addressed many of the things the employer is looking for. In the interview, you need to focus on all the criteria, but they are not all weighted equally. It is not just your skills that will make an impact on the interviewer. Let's look at the criteria. This is how you will be evaluated.

Job Qualifications. You are qualified. You are screened on the basis of your cover letter and resumé. Why would you get an interview if you were not qualified? You are entering the job market for the first time and you don't have any experience. The employer knows this. You are looking for and entry-level position. Your education and resumé got you to the interview.

You don't have to spend much time in the interview telling the interviewer about your qualifications. They know them.

Image and Appearance. This is important to every employer because you must fit the company image. The employer will be looking at you to determine if you can represent the company the way they want. Your first impression, dress code and the overall way you present yourself will be under scrutiny. This should not be a problem if you use good judgment and prepare correctly.

Communication Skills. Every job will require you to communicate with people. Writing and verbal skills are important. Your cover letter, your resumé, your phone conversations during the hiring process all give you a chance to demonstrate your communication skills. They are all important.

By the time you get to the interview, the interviewer has probably already drawn some conclusions about your communication skills.

Attitude and Motivation. This is the single most important part of the interviewing process. If you cannot convince the employer you really want the job, why would they hire you? You must convince the employer you want the job. But of course you want the job. You still need to prove it to the interviewer. Every contact you have with the employer gives you an opportunity to show your enthusiasm and motivation. Again during the interview, this should be your number-one objective.

Be certain to tell them you really want the job. You must convince the interviewer you are serious about the opportunity.

> *"YOUR ATTITUDE, NOT YOUR APTITUDE,*
> *WILL DETERMINE YOUR ALTITUDE."*
> *ZIG ZIGLAR*

YOUR INTERVIEW STARTS WITH "THE CALL."

"THANK YOU FOR YOUR COVER LETTER AND RESUMÉ. WE WOULD LIKE YOU TO COME IN FOR AN INTERVIEW NEXT FRIDAY AT 2:00 P.M."

You have been networking, sending out your resumé, following up on all your leads and finally, you get "the call."

Now what?

Interview Checklist

Upon receiving "the call" scheduling your interview, either ask or phone back to:

- Thank them for their call and express your enthusiasm about the opportunity.

- Confirm, time, date and location of the interview.

- Confirm the full name and title of the interviewer (Be certain you know how to correctly pronounce the name of the interviewer and/or people you are going to meet. Not sure? Call the receptionist to ask.)

- Ask if there is a job description. If there is, you want to see it. If there isn't, you will be acknowledged for your professionalism and enthusiasm just for asking.

- Ask if there is anything specific you should bring to the interview (references, portfolio..etc.)

Start your pre-interview preparation by:

- **Confirming.** The length of time it will take to get to the interview... How will you get there?…Where will you park? Remember, you *do not* want to be late.

- **Confirming.** All the phone numbers of the company and interviewer.

- **Setting goals for the interview.** What do you want the interviewer to know about you? How will you work this into the conversation?

- **Researching the position.** What knowledge, skills, and abilities are required for success in this position? Think about your past experiences, volunteer work, full-time and temp work, internships, clubs, and associations to determine how they are applicable.

- **Researching the company.** What is the culture of this company? Gather information from the company's annual report, their website, as well as newspaper and magazine articles, etc.
Will you fit into this culture?

- **Researching the interviewer and interview location.** Know the proper spelling and pronunciation of the interviewer's name. Know the interviewer's position (manager, human resources specialist, etc.). Know where the interview will take place and how to get there.

- **Reviewing your resumé.** What does the interviewer already know about you? What information needs to be clarified or explained in more detail? What do you want to highlight?

- **Practicing the answers to all interview questions you could be asked.** Prepare an outline of your answers. Write them down. Practice your responses out loud. Relate answers to information on your resumé.

- **Preparing your questions to ask.** Have several questions ready that will show your interest, your preparation and your knowledge of the company and industry.

- **Preparing and rehearsing your opening speech.**

- **Preparing and rehearsing your closing, "I want this job" speech.**

The Day Before Interview

- **Always call to confirm interview.** Even if you only leave a voice-mail with the employer confirming your interview, you are showing them you are organized, professional and enthusiastic.
    ...message."Mr./Ms. Smith, it's Mark Wicken calling to confirm my interview with you tomorrow at 2:00 p.m. I am very excited about this opportunity and look forward to meeting with you."

- **Prepare an interview pack.** Plan to bring a portfolio or briefcase (NOT a backpack!). Include a notepad and pen, directions to the interview, extra copies of your resumé and references, and your portfolio (if applicable).

- **Plan your outfit.** Dress professionally, even if the job is casual. Choose conservative styles and colors. Clothing should be clean and neat. Best advice? Wear something that makes you feel good. If you feel good, you will be confident.

- **Get a good night's sleep.** By this point, you are well prepared. Don't stay up late rehearsing questions and answers. Instead, get a good night's sleep so you look fresh and alert. If you show up for an interview after a night of partying...the interviewer will be able to tell.

The Interview Day

- Remember, you never get a second chance to make a first impression. Be early...not just on time. Arrive ahead of time (15 minutes minimum) but never late.

GREAT IDEA!
Consider writing down a few of the questions you would like to ask the interviewer or some of the points you want to be sure you tell about yourself on your notepad. Will this show that you are prepared and enthusiastic? You bet!

- Turn off your cell phone...even better, don't take it into the interview.

- Do not to bring a coffee or beverage with you into the reception area or the interview.

- Be polite to the receptionist...you just might be working there soon.

- When you are waiting in the reception area, look around, observe
  what is going on, listen.

- Meet the interviewer with a firm handshake, eye contact and an appropriate greeting using his or her proper name, (Mr. or Ms.).

- Always know what you are going to say…"Your opening speech,"

- **SMILE!**
  Nothing says I am really happy to meet you like a smile. You should be happy and excited…this could be the person who hires you.

GREAT IDEA!
Before the interview even starts, while walking to the interview room, thank the interviewer for the opportunity to meet with them and tell them how excited you are about the possibility of working for them. Another "Remember Me!"

"UNLESS AN AUDIENCE (THE INTERVIEWER)
SEES THE RIGHT IMAGE,
IT DOESN'T HEAR THE RIGHT MESSAGE."
MARK BOWDEN

Remember. You are *giving* an interview not *taking* one. If you are not there to speak about yourself, don't bother going. Your job interview is nothing more than a structured conversation between two people hoping to discover they have something in common.

(SEE EXHIBIT 7 FOR YOUR INTERVIEW CHECKLIST)

Giving a great interview may not only just start your career, it could change your life forever if you get the job you really want.

The First Five Minutes

The first five minutes of your interview are critical and often the interviewer will have made up his or her mind about you before you even think the interview has started. By this time the interviewer will have noted:

- **Writing Skills** - from your cover letter and resumé

- **Telephone and communications skills** - from your phone messages and conversations

- **Organizational skills** - from your confirmation phone call the day before the interview

- **Punctuality** - arriving early for the interview

- **Appearance and grooming** - your professional appearance

- **Eye contact** - showing your confidence

- **Handshake** - showing your confidence

- **Use of names** - showing respect for the interviewer's position

- **Body language** - showing your confidence

- **Articulation and tone of voice** - showing good verbal skills

- **Opening speech** - showing your enthusiasm and motivation

Before the interviewer has asked you *one* question, your pre-interview behavior has shown you are professional, organized, prepared, enthusiastic, personable, polite and motivated. A good start? You bet! Another "Remember Me!"

Interview Questions Are Designed To Determine Three Things...

- **Can you do the job?** The answer to the first question is "yes." You are right out of school. They know your qualifications. Why would a company interview you if they did not think you were qualified? You can do the job. You are qualified...that's why you are in the interview.

- **Will you fit in the company?** Will you fit in? This is a judgment call based on personal chemistry and the way you behave in the interview. The interviewer will want to know if you are the kind of person they would like to work with and the kind others would like to work with.

- **Do you want the job?** This is the reason you are there. Your answers to all questions must convince the interviewer you can make a contribution and that you want the job.

The person conducting the interview has a responsibility to his or her company.
Their role is to hire the best possible person for the job. The reality is that the interviewer's own job might depend on it.
("...if I hire the right person, the one who turns out to be a great employee, I get to keep my job. If I hire a person who turns out to be a poor employee maybe I'll get the blame for hiring them.")

The secret to answering every interview question is to understand what the interviewer wants and needs to hear.

**Here is *absolutely* the best way
to respond to all the questions.**

Answer every question as if the interviewer says, after the question...
"...and what is in it for me?"

By answering each question with this in mind you will be giving the interviewer all the reasons to conclude you are the right person for the job. The interviewer is looking for ways to eliminate the average candidate.

You must turn a common question into a memorable answer that is meaningful to the interviewer and gives them a reason to hire you.

REMEMBER ME!

The Most Common Questions You Will Be Asked

- **"Tell Me About Yourself. Who Are You? Why Do You Want This Job?"** The first question in most interviews gives you a chance to use your "elevator speech" which states your current situation and your passion for the industry.

- **"What are your career goals? Long-term goals? etc…"** This type of question gives you another chance to talk about your passion for the business and desire to be a part of the company. The best answer is to say…"working for you with newly acquired skills and growing responsibilities, and to be recognized for making a valuable contribution to the success of your company."

- **"What is your greatest accomplishment? What are you most proud of?"** The interviewer is hoping you are going to say "graduating"…Isn't that why you are here. Being proud of your academic achievements should be at the top of your list.

- **"What are your strengths?"** If you have done your homework and know what the interviewer is looking for, talk about your transferable skills that best relate to the job.

- **"What are your weaknesses?"** (Trick question) You don't have any or at least for what they are looking for you don't have any. Answer: "I have reviewed your job description and am confident I have the qualifications you are looking for."

- **"What do you know about our company?"**
  This is a **BIG** one.
  If you don't know anything about the company, why are you there? If you have done your homework you should know something "current" about the company and their business. (Do not just feed back information that is on their web site. They know that.) They want to know if you have made any effort to learn more about the company and their business. If you haven't made the effort they will label you…"DO NOT HIRE."

- **"Why do you want to work here?"** Here is another chance for you to tell the interviewer about your passion for the business. DO NOT tell the interviewer you "want to get experience". Similar to your resumé, this language is the kiss of death in an interview. No one is going to hire you so you can get experience and then move on to another job.
  DO NOT say you are looking for a new challenge. It will sound like you bore easily.

- **"Why did you choose to go to (your college/ university)?"** The interviewer is trying to find out when your interest in the business or industry started. Perhaps you developed an interest while at school. They are trying to figure out if you want a career or are just looking for a job.

- **"What are your salary expectations?"** This is always a difficult question to answer. Should you state a number too high and be out of the running? Should you state a number too low and undervalue yourself? The reality is that they know exactly what they are going to offer you. Remember, this is an entry-level position and you don't have a lot to negotiate with. They want to know if your expectations are realistic. You should probably know before you go to the interview what the range will be for your industry. If you don't, just say you expect to be paid fairly for the entry-level position.

- **"You are one of many qualified candidates...why should we hire you?"** Here is your opportunity to tell the interviewer your passion for the business and your desire to use your education, skills and experience to make a contribution to the company.

(SEE EXHIBIT 8 FOR A COMPLETE LIST OF QUESTIONS YOU MIGHT EXPECT)

Remember, the purpose of every question is to give you a chance to talk about something you care about and something you want the interviewer to know about you.

**Anything that *can* be misunderstood *will* be misunderstood.
You must have all the answers.**

Best Questions For Graduates To Ask In An Interview

Having no questions is the worst thing you can do in your interview. At some point in every interview the interviewer will ask: "Do you have any questions?" If your answer is "No" be assured that the interview is over and you will not get the job.

The reason? By answering "No" you are telling the interviewer you are not really interested in the job or the company and/or you did not prepare properly for the interview. Either way you have ruined any chance of getting the job.

Come to every interview with a set of questions that shows the interviewer you are prepared, you are interested and you really want the job.

Interviewers like candidates who ask thoughtful, intelligent questions about the company and the job because it shows you have done your homework. Here are some of the best.

- **"Please tell me more about the position and the kind of person you are looking for?"** The answer to this question will give you one more chance to assure the interviewer you have the qualities they are looking for.

- **"Is this a new position or am I replacing someone?"** The answer will tell you why you are being hired. If it is a new position…good, the company is growing. If it is replacing someone, you can find out what happened to that person. Promoted, resigned, let go. Important to know… Right?

- **"Who would I be reporting to?"** You must know who your immediate superior is going to be. This will most likely be the person who will train you and determine if you are doing a good job.

- **"What are the criteria against which my performance will be judged?"** You need to know how you will be evaluated and what are the criteria for success on this job. Otherwise, how will you know how to behave?

- **"When I do a good job for you, will there be a chance for advancement?"** You are telling the interviewer you are confident you will do a good job and that you what to be a part of the growth of the company.

- **"What will be my greatest challenge in this position?"** You are telling the interviewer you know there are expectations of you and you want to know what you need to do to be successful.

- **"How did you (the interviewer) get started in the business?"** People like to talk about themselves and this question shows you are interested in the interviewer's comments and opinions.

- **"Could you tell me what a typical day would be like for me?"** This question makes the assumption you will get hired, shows confidence and an interest in working for them.

- **"I have read about (some current information about the company or industry)…can you tell me more?"** This type of question shows you have done your homework, know something about the company or industry and are interested in their business.

- **"I am excited and confident about the possibility of working for you. What are the next steps in your selection process?"** You must know what the next steps are so you will know how and when to follow up. This will show your organizational skills, your interest and enthusiasm.

THE BEST FOR LAST.
There is one question, if asked correctly, could be the deal-maker in your interview.
Ask…

"Is there anything I can say or do between now and the time you make your final decision to convince you that I am the right person for this job?"

By asking this question, in this way, you are challenging the interviewer to ask you any questions they may feel you have not answered. It also says you are sincere about your intentions, and confident and eager to work there. Most importantly you are telling the interviewer you want the job.

> **What is the downside? Nothing.**
> **What is the upside? They just might 'Remember' you because you asked great questions.**
> **Another "Remember Me!"**

Remember, in order to ask relevant questions, you need to do your research on the company. These questions are just examples to give you an idea of the kinds of things you could ask.

Not all these questions are appropriate for every job opportunity or interview. Prepare your questions carefully. But remember, nothing sounds worse than asking an inappropriate question or one that indicates you have not done your homework. Be prepared.

The Closer

Interviewers remember what they hear first and what they hear last. You made a great impression with your "opening speech."

It's now time to close. You will know when the interview is coming to a close and you should be ready with your "closing speech."

You must convince the interviewer you are seriously interested. If you don't tell the interviewer directly, do not assume they will conclude you are interested.

Interviewers cannot read your mind. Ask for the job.

Close by saying... *"Thank you for taking time to meet with me. After hearing more about this position and talking with you, I am convinced more than ever I have the right qualifications, passion and enthusiasm to do a great job for you. Please consider me seriously for this position...I really want this job."*

Another BIG "Remember Me!"

Tips For Answering Interview Questions

- Be prepared to answer typical interview questions.

- Listen carefully to the question before answering, and if you do not understand the question ask for clarification.

- Think about what you want to include in your response to the question before you begin to speak.

- Keep a positive attitude at all times.

- Answer honestly at all times.

- Always stress your successes and avoid any negative comments or complaints about previous jobs or previous bosses.

- Keep answers short and ask if your response answers the question. Remain focused and do not ramble or give unnecessary information.

- Maintain eye contact, project your voice and be aware of proper posture.

- Show a sincere interest in the company and position.

- Express yourself clearly and with confidence, without conceit.

- Convey enthusiasm, and a sense of pride in your education and accomplishments.

- Focus on what you can contribute to the organization rather than what the employer can do for you.

- Close the interview on an assumptive note. Indicate the job looks like a good fit and you feel you can make a contribution to the organization. End by asking about the next steps and telling them you want the job.

Interview Don'ts

There are some subjects you should not raise in an interview.
Don't ask about vacation time, sick days or how long lunch-time is. These questions will only turn off the employer. Until you are offered the job none of these matter. Focus on what you have to offer, your talent, education and enthusiasm for the job.

- **Don't** talk about personal or family issues or difficulties.

- **Don't** talk about travel plans or additional school plans.

- **Don't** say, "When do I start?" Some graduates think this shows confidence. No, it sounds arrogant.

- **Never** say one of your objectives is to start your own business. If you have to ask why, think again.

- **Never** say your are looking to get experience. You will be hired to make a contribution to the company, not for them to give you experience.

> **If you do not show the interviewer that your are interested, excited and passionate about the job, how can you expect the interviewer to feel excited about hiring you?**

Reasons Graduates Are Rejected After The Interview

- **Poor interview manners.**
  Never arrive late...the fatal mistake. Always shake hands, smile and make eye contact.

- **Poor appearance.**
  First impressions are lasting impressions. Always dress for the position. An employer might reason that the person who doesn't care about their appearance will not care about the job.

- **Unrealistic demands about the job.**
  Talk about the opportunities to learn and contribute, and show your enthusiasm to work.

- **Knowing little about the company.**
  Learn as much as you can about the company before the interview. Have questions prepared.

- **Salary requests.**
  Do not raise the question of salary or benefits in the interview. Let the interviewer raise the subject. This is not a guessing game. They know what they are going to pay you.

- **Talking too much in the interview.**
  Learn to listen. Make your point and listen to their response.

- **Talking too little in the interview.**
  Answer questions fully and give all the information requested. You are there to talk about you.

- **Being too charming.**
  Don't try to be too clever or act superficial.

- **Being too modest.**
  Don't be afraid to blow your own horn.
  Talk about your accomplishments, awards etc.

- **Not telling the interviewer that you want the job.**
  This is the reason you are there. Right? Be sure to tell them or they may conclude you are not interested.

- **Lack of follow-up.**
  Ask when you can expect to hear from them. Ask if you can follow up after an appropriate period of time. After the interview (every interview) write a "Thank-you" note.

Summary Of The Steps For Interview Success

Prepare, Prepare, Prepare

- Research the industry, market and prospective employer thoroughly.

- Approach from the perspective of the person doing the hiring. What is that person be looking for?

- Plan responses to information you want them to know about you.

- Rehearse all your responses out loud. Practice your answers in front of a mirror.

- Prepare a brief summary of your background that answers the questions: "Tell me about yourself? Who are you?"

- Memorize all the timelines on your resumé.

Attitude Makes The Difference

- Employers are looking for people with a positive work attitude.

- Display confidence by speaking authoritatively about your accomplishments without appearing arrogant.

- Emphasize your personal qualities, values and behavior that demonstrate your cultural fit.

Ask The Right Questions

- Ask about the position, job responsibilities and company values. Don't just tell them about you.

Dress For Success

- Find out the dress code before the interview.

- Over-dress rather than under-dress. Business casual is usually a safe bet.

- Dress in clothing that makes you feel good. If you feel good you will look good.

Leave A Lasting "Remember Me!" Impression

- Impress everyone you encounter, including the receptionist, secretary or administrative assistant.

- Follow up the interview with a "Thank-you" letter response. It is your last chance to reinforce why you are the right person and why they should hire you.

- Tell them "I want this job" and tell them why!

**Companies like candidates who have done their homework and are prepared for the interview.
They will conclude that someone who works hard to *get the job* will work hard *on the job*.**

Interview Etiquette Counts

Business and interview etiquette is extremely important. It shows you know how to handle yourself in important situations. After all, your first interview might be the most important interview in your career. Treat it like it is. It could be the one that gets you in the door.

Poor etiquette suggests poor judgment.

Points to Consider

- Always arrive early.

- Your demeanor comes under scrutiny right from the beginning – the moment you walk in the door.

- Your first impression means everything

- Be courteous to the receptionists. They are the gatekeepers.

- Smile, it shows confidence.

- Leave your cell phone in your purse or briefcase – TURNED OFF.

- Don't be chewing gum, eating, drinking.

- Wait for the interviewer to sit down before you do.

- Don't address the interviewer by his/her first name unless told to.

- Listen to the interviewer carefully. It shows you are really interested.

- You are making a presentation. Know what you want to say. Practice.

- Maintain eye contact throughout the interview, sit up straight, no slouching, and speak clearly.

- When you are on an interview, focus 100%. Put everything else out of your mind.

"OUTCLASSING THE COMPETITION IS THE NAME OF THE GAME IF YOU WANT TO SURVIVE ...GOOD MANNERS ARE GOOD BUSINESS."
HILKA KLINKENBERG,

Remember…
The person who gets the job
is the person who *"aces"* **the interview.**
Period!

If You Smoke, Don't Be Surprised You Don't Get The Job.

For all you smokers out there, I am not going to discuss the reasons why you shouldn't smoke. You know them. For graduates who do smoke don't be surprised if you don't get the job.

Here Are The Reasons:

FACT: Most people don't smoke.

FACT: People who don't smoke are usually turned off by the smell of smoke and smokers.

FACT: If you are a smoker, you smell like smoke. You might not think so, but you do. The smell is on your clothes and on your breath. It is hard to get off or cover up.

FACT: Smokers are more prone to sickness and take more sick days than non-smokers.

FACT: When you are home sick, you are not being productive.

FACT: If you are not at work, you are costing your employer money.

FACT: Smoke breaks have a negative impact on productivity.

FACT: If you are on the job and you are sick, you are probably not being productive and most likely making others sick.

REALITY: If an employer has a choice to hire a smoker or a non-smoker...

Who do you think they will hire?

The Telephone Interview

There may be a situation when a telephone interview is part of the process. Companies use the telephone interview more and more today because it can reduce recruiting time, save money and often "weed out" inappropriate candidates just by evaluating their communication skills.

Remember, a phone interview may be the first contact with a potential employer and it can happen any time and often be unannounced.

Your goal will be to get a face-to-face interview. Always be ready for a telephone interview and follow these steps:

- Remember, the telephone interview starts with the sound of your voice...a first impression. Always answer your phone politely.

- Be sure you are in a quiet room.

- Smile when you speak and stand up when you talk. It removes pressure from your diaphragm and your voice will sound better.

- Remember, the interviewer cannot see you so you can keep a copy of your resumé by the phone and have a pen and paper in hand to make notes. Also, have any notes about the company ready by your phone if you are anticipating a phone interview.

- Listen to every question carefully and answer them just like in a face to face interview situation.

- If you get called on your cell phone and it is not convenient to talk, ask for the information of the caller and return the call as soon as possible from a more appropriate location.

- Do not eat, drink or chew gum during the conversation and never put the interviewer on hold.

- Always follow up after the call with a "Thank-you" note just like in a face-to-face interview.

A good phone interview could be your ticket to a face-to-face interview.

Your Interview Strategy

Remember, this is your interview which means you are not taking an interview, you are "giving" an interview.

If you go to the interview and are not prepared to give information and share your enthusiasm for the position...don't bother to show up.

Keep in mind that every question you are asked gives you the chance to talk about what you think is important for the interviewer to know about you. You don't have experience. They know that. They are probably not interested in your opinions but more in how you think and how you behave in certain situations.

Remember, this is an interview, not a friendly chat, so everything you say is important and on the record.

If your responses to the questions are not interesting and meaningful to the interviewer, it is *your* fault, not the interviewer's.

After the interview you cannot say, they never asked me the right questions. It is up to you to tell them what you want them to know about you and why they should consider hiring you.

**They will not hire you
if they do not remember you.**

Final Interview Advice For Graduates

Companies like candidates who know what they want.

Make every effort to know everything you can about the company you are interviewing with. The candidate who shows the most interest in the company and convinces them they want the job...usually gets it.

Your job is to sell yourself to the interviewer. Do not treat your interview casually. You cannot over-prepare. You cannot practice too much.

One important key to a great interview is self confidence. An important key to self confidence is preparation.

If you make a good first impression, answer all the questions clearly, ask intelligent questions of the interviewer and follow up effectively...there is a pretty good chance you will get the job. Why? because there is a good chance your competition won't

REMEMBER ME!

The single most important thing that you must do at the end of the interview is to tell the interviewer..."**I WANT THIS JOB.**"

Use these words or your words and there will be no doubt in the interviewer's mind that you want the job. The slightest doubt will eliminate you from consideration and other possible opportunities that could result from the interview.

You are probably asking yourself how you can tell them you want the job without sounding like you are desperate. It is not hard. In your closing speech (which of course you will have prepared and rehearsed) find language like this:

"Mr/Ms Smith, thank you for your time today. After hearing about the position and your company I am convinced more than ever that I am the right person for this job and I want you to know I am sincerely interested in this opportunity."

This simple act of telling the interviewer you want the job is in itself a "point of difference" that will differentiate you from most of your competition.

What is the downside?....nothing.

What is the upside?... They just might hire you.

Another "Remember Me!"

Chapter Summary

1. Clearly, when you get an interview you are qualified. Why would someone interview you if you were not qualified? Your job will be to convince the interviewer you are the right fit and you want the job

2. Answer every interview question as if the interviewer is asking: "What is in it for me?...Why is this important to me?"

3. Be absolutely certain that you tell the interviewer you want the job. Have your closing speech ready. This could be the most important speech or pitch you ever make. It just might get you the job.

Interviewers cannot read your mind.
If you do not tell the interviewer "specifically" that you want the job, he /she very well might think you are not interested.

Your choice!

Chapter 8

YOUR FOLLOW-UP AFTER THE INTERVIEW

"IT'S NOT OVER 'TILL IT'S OVER."
YOGI BERRA

YOUR POST-INTERVIEW STRATEGY

The interview is not over when you walk out the door. You still have many opportunities to continue your **"Remember Me!"** strategy.

Your "Thank-you" Letter

A "Thank-you" letter is far too often the one component of the job-search process most graduates leave out. Sometimes it is forgotten, not thought to be important or not sent because of disinterest in the position after the interview.

No matter what the reasons, it is a BIG mistake not to send a "Thank-you" letter after *every* interview.

The purpose of the "Thank-you" letter:

- To thank the interviewer for their time and the interview,

- To get the attention of the interviewer one more time,

- To show you paid attention to the interviewer and understood their comments.

- To restate your interest and enthusiasm for the position.

- To restate your strengths and the reasons you think you are appropriate for the position,

    ...and besides, it is good manners.

The "Thank-you" letter is another **"Remember Me!"** in the long list you have created throughout this whole job-search process.

By not following-up after the interview you could be telling the interviewer you are not interested in the position. When the moment of truth comes and the interviewer has to decide who to hire, if you haven't sent a follow-up, they may conclude (and incorrectly so) you are not interested.
Even if you are not sure the job is right for you, until they offer you the position you do not have to say "no."

There may be other possibilities or future opportunities with the company you are not aware of. If you don't follow up after the interview you are indirectly telling them you really were not interested in the first place. Is this the impression you want to leave?

Always, follow up after every interview with everyone you have met. The first interview follow-up should be with a "personal" hard copy letter or note right after the interview. Subsequent follow-ups could be either a letter, email or voice-mail. Your choice.

Your goal is to differentiate yourself from the competition and be remembered. The "Thank-you" note is the one part of this process most people dismiss for all the wrong reasons. It can be a deal maker.

What is the downside?...Nothing.

What is the upside?...

They just might remember you.

Another "Remember Me!"

DISAPPOINTMENT!

"You did not get the job."

Do not be surprised if you don't get the first job you interview for. It happens sometimes. (Sorry it does.) This does not mean you will never get a job. It means someone else did a better job at their job search than you did...So now what?

Just because you didn't get hired does not mean you did not leave a great impression. Once you have been notified you were not successful, be sure to follow up (once again) with everyone you met during the process, thanking them for the opportunity to have met with them...expressing interest in any other positions that might come in the future.

This is a "great" strategy. It keeps the door open and continues your networking process.

Depending on the relationship you may have developed during the interview process, you may choose to contact the interviewer for advice on what you might have done better in the interview and ask for referrals to others in the industry.

Job search is about building relationships. If you make a good impression you will see returns in the future. Guaranteed!

A professional, sincere, well-crafted letter of thanks to the company and persons with whom you had interviews, even if you did not get the job, will show how professional you really are and, most importantly, leave the door open for the future.

What is the downside?...Nothing.
What is the upside?...
They just might remember you

"FAILURE DOESN'T MEAN YOU ARE A FAILURE, IT JUST MEANS YOU HAVEN'T SUCCEEDED YET."
ROBERT H. SCHULLER

SUCCESS!
"You Got The Job!"

The interviews are over, you have been given a job offer and you have accepted...CONGRATULATIONS!

What Are You Going To Do Now????

Besides celebrating...and you should, you now have a chance to show everyone you met that you really are a professional.

During this job-search process you will have met many people, interviewed with many companies and spoken to many about your search.

It is now time to thank everyone and **TELL EVERYONE** you have been successful.

Yes!... EVERYONE!

This could be the smartest career decision you ever make. Why? By thanking all those who helped along the way, everyone you approached and everyone you met, you are telling them you are now one of them. You are in the business.

This may seem uncomfortable at first. Why would you contact those companies that didn't hire you or those people who didn't even return your calls or answer your job applications?

Why? Because there is a good chance sometime in the future you might be looking for another job or someone to network with.

Besides...if you left the right impression, when they hear from you most people will think "Good for you..I am happy for you!"

**What is the downside?...Nothing.
What is the upside?...People will know where you are working, and you end up building that all-important network that you will have the rest of your career.
Another "Remember Me!"**

Tell everyone you know you have a job

...and be proud of it.

You earned it.

(It's called advertising)

Chapter Summary

1   A "Thank-you" letter is critical to job-search success because it lets the potential employer know you are interested and it can reinforce the reasons to hire you.

2   Even if you don't get the job (the first time) always thank the interviewer and the company for their time. You might be next in line.

3   Always contact every person you will have met and everyone who helps you in your job search to let them know your success. This is your network.
This is your future. Keep in touch.

Chapter 9

NOW YOU HAVE THE JOB!

"WHAT YOU GET BY ACHIEVING YOUR GOALS IS NOT AS IMPORTANT AS WHAT YOU BECOME BY ACHIEVING YOUR GOALS."
ZIG ZIGLAR

Tips For Starting Your New Job

When you start your new job it will be an exciting time. Here are some tips to help you to move forward confidently and get off to a good start.

- **Be early and don't leave early.** It will be noticed.

- **Get to know people.** First, meet people in your department and then people in departments you work with. Listen more than you talk. Ask lots of questions and get clarification if necessary so you truly understand how the agency/department/business works.

- **Ask questions**...there are no stupid questions. Asking questions doesn't make you look stupid, it makes you look and be smart.

- **Realize that you know nothing.** Don't be afraid to admit you don't know something - it's your greatest safety net and your greatest opportunity. Be a sponge and soak up everything around you.

- **Listen more and talk less.** You learn more when you are listening than when you are talking.

- **Don't try to change everything at once.** Be open to learning "their" way before you suggest "your" way.

- **Get in sync with your boss's priorities.** What are his/her expectations of you? Make sure you are living up to them.

- **Have lunch with different people in the organization.** Learn the "unwritten rules" of your new workplace.

- **Learn about the culture.** Seek out those people who have been there a long time and meet with them.

- **Get to know the key players.** Seek out people both inside and outside your area who have roles that are critical to your team's success. Ask for their support and offer yours to them.

- **Take care of yourself.** Create a schedule for yourself that includes time off and good self-care. New jobs are stressful, so include activities that you know reduce stress for you, example: proper rest, exercise, good diet, family time, etc.

- **Celebrate your success!** Feel good about what you have accomplished. Confidence is an important part of success.

- **Work hard.** Learn your craft. Immerse yourself in it.

- **Play nicely.** You can be the most talented person in your company but if you cannot master the people skills you will go nowhere. If you cannot interact with your boss, peers, etc., you're doomed.

- **Have a sense of urgency.** Everything is needed yesterday. Be ahead of the curve, plan and anticipate.

- **Use the 'We' word a lot.** You didn't create your ideas in isolation, many people contributed. Be a team player.

- **Make your clients love you.** If a client likes working with you, they will trust you and give you the benefit of the doubt when you need it.

- **Learn to be a great presenter.** It is one thing to have great ideas and another thing to sell them. Learn to present your ideas clearly.

- **Be organized.** Be more organized than everyone else. Learn to manage timetables and budgets.

- **Pick your battles.** You cannot "go to the wall" every time. Give in on things that honestly do not matter.

- **Keep your perspective.** When someone kills your idea, no one will die. Develop a tough skin. You will need it.

- **Be curious.** Read everything you can about your business. Be a student of your business and the world. Be aware of news, trends and cultures.

- **Smile and be friendly.** It's hard to like or work with someone who is not happy and friendly.

- **Keep a sense of humor**. If you don't laugh you will go insane. Have fun. After all, this is what you wanted.

- **And...**

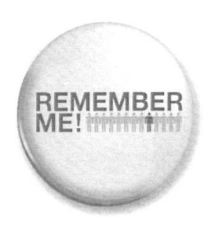

Don't forget to keep building your REMEMBER ME! moments.

Things They Didn't Tell You At School

Now that you have graduated and landed you first job, the voyage has started. The safe haven of the classroom has now become the reality of your first job...Lots to learn and lots of challenges ahead.

Now, the "real-world" education kicks in and it will be a greater learning curve that you could ever imagine. You will be tested on your work and deadlines every day. You are not paid or rewarded for effort. You are paid for results.

Your performance in school impacted only you, nobody else. In stark contrast, your performance at work impacts your company, your bosses and your co-workers.

Here are some thoughts to help you make the transition from graduate to a successful career.

- **Shift your focus from "I" to "We."** Throughout your school years the focus has been on you. Basically, you picked and chose what to do and when to do it. Now the person who pays you controls that. Think "we" and what you can contribute to the good of the company and you will be on the right track.

- **Etiquette Counts.** Your every behavior will be noticed. "Please and Thank-you" are still the best words in the English language. Be polite, be punctual, dress appropriately, and avoid office gossip.

- **People first.** Your ability to get along with the people you work with and for will be the key to your success and happiness in your career. You don't choose your co-workers, but your ability to work with them is what you are being paid to do. Learn to be tolerant and cooperative. Likable and pleasant to work with beats a bad attitude every time. People skills count.

- **Ask questions.** Asking questions and taking advice isn't a sign of weakness. Seeking ways to improve yourself is a sign of maturity. When you are new on the job there are no poor or dumb questions. Pay attention, observe and learn from the experienced people around you. It is better to learn by asking questions than by making mistakes.

- **Networking never ends.** Most likely it was your networking that played a part in you landing your first job. Your network will unquestionably help you navigate the rest of your career. Keep networking. You can never have enough contacts in your business network.

- **Write really well.** Develop your skill with written communications to the highest level in everything you write (including emails). Often your written communication will be a first impression and will show you are capable and intelligent.

- **Learn to be a great presenter.** The ability to stand up and make a presentation might be the single most important business skill you will ever learn. If you cannot present your ideas, who will?

- **Keep your resumé current.** You cannot know when the next opportunity will present itself or, worst case, when something will happen at your job that forces you to move quickly to another opportunity. Make sure your resumé is always updated with promotions and accomplishments.

- **Avoid acting like an idiot.** Too often talented people "shoot themselves in the foot" by stupid habits, improper attire, being late, inappropriate jokes or language, etc. You need to prove you can follow the rules before you can get away with breaking them. It's hard to earn respect when you've been fired. Exercise good judgment always.

- **Appreciate the people who help you.** Never burn bridges. It is a small world and you need all the friends and support you can get. Those who helped you get your job and those you work with will always be your safety net if you treat them right.

"THE BEST WAY TO APPRECIATE YOUR JOB IS TO IMAGINE YOURSELF WITHOUT ONE."
OSCAR WILDE

Things I'm Glad Someone Told Me!

About Business...

- Learn to remember names.
- Learn to write business letters and "Thank-you" letters.
- Learn how to make a proper introductions.
- Read business and trade publications about your business.
- Take a time management course and develop your own system.
- Send "Thank-you" notes and acknowledge people who help you.
- Say "Please" and "Thank-you" a lot.

About Personal Behavior...

- Never, ever tell a lie. If you tell the truth you don't have to have a good memory.
- If you tell a racist joke in the office, don't be surprised if you get fired.
- If you tell an off-color joke, don't be surprised if you get fired.
- Being good is important, being trusted is essential.
- Never say, "It's not my job."
- Don't promise what you cannot deliver.

- If you don't know the answer, just say so. Then find the answer.

- Assume no one can or will keep a secret.

- Be honest with yourself about your strengths and weakness.

- Don't tell people their ideas are bad unless you have a better one.

- Don't talk about your boss, client or projects in elevators or taxis

About Career Path...

- If you interview for another job, expect your boss to find out.

- Keep an accurate mailing list of all the people in your business.

- Always have an answer to the question, "What would I do if I lost my job tomorrow?"

- Don't surround yourself with people just like you. Strive for difference and diversity.

- If a job sounds too good to be true, it probably is.

- If you are worried about your job...you probably should be.

- Past performance is the best indicator of future performance, not just for you but for your boss and company as well.

About The Job...

- Never take a problem to your boss without some solutions.

- Don't be late for meetings.

- Never, ever miss deadlines.

- Be prepared for performance reviews and ask for them.

- Long hours don't mean anything. Results count, not effort.

- Always know how you are doing on your job? Ask.

"IT'S NOT WHAT WE DO ONCE IN A WHILE THAT SHAPES OUR LIVES.
IT'S WHAT WE DO CONSISTENTLY."
ANTHONY ROBBINS

Chapter Summary

1. The single most important ingredient in the formula for success is knowing how to get along with people. Behave professionally and cultivate good relationships with everyone you meet.

2. Now that you have a job, remember that you are being paid for results, not effort. Work hard, ask questions, and never stop learning about your profession.

3. Success is simple. Do what you know is right, the right way, at the right time. Your attitude determines your altitude.

Chapter 10

YOUR TIME MANAGEMENT

IF YOU ARE NOT MANAGING YOUR TIME...WHO IS? HOW YOU USE YOUR TIME IS YOUR CHOICE.

TIME MANAGEMENT

One of the most important skills you will need in your job search and when you start to work, will be time management.

While in school your time was most likely controlled by your parents and your school. No one had to tell you when to get up in the morning, when to show up to class, when to hand in an assignment. All this was dictated to you and if you followed the rules you usually accomplished what you were suppose to accomplish.

If you have good time management skills it will make your job search easier and more effective and you will take those skills into the job market.

If you don't have good time management skills, no doubt, be a problem for you. Most employers will be looking for this skill so they do not have to teach you. You can demonstrate this skill throughout the job-search process.

What Is Time Management?

- The ability to manage your time

- The ability to manage your personal life

- The ability to manage your business (school) life

- The ability to help manage other people's time

- The ability to accomplish what you want to do, when you want to

Effective time management is the art and science of getting control over the entire 24 hours, in every day.

The reality is that you cannot manage time - you can only manage yourself in relation to time. Time management is all about self management. It is important that you approach the idea of time management and your attitude towards it properly.

Often our negative attitudes make excuses so we don't address the real issue of our self management:

- "Where did the time go?" …It is not my fault I couldn't get the assignment done.

- "I never have time to"…versus I chose not to.

- "One of these days"…I don't have to worry because I will do it later.

- "I'm too busy to"…versus I did not use my time wisely.

- "I just didn't have or wasn't given enough time"…It was someone else's fault…versus I used my time poorly.

Time Management and Successful People

If you want to be successful at what you do, it makes sense to look at people who are successful and see what they do and how they have behaved to reach their level of success. No matter what your definition of success, there are certain things we can say about successful people.

Key traits that successful people have in common:

- They enjoy their work
- They have a positive attitude and are confident
- They use negative experiences to learn
- They are decisive and disciplined goal setters
- They are persistent and consistent
- They have good communication skills
- They are healthy, with high energy levels
- They surround themselves with supportive people

What do we often say about successful people?

- They are clear about what they want
- They get things done, even things they may not really want to do
- They accomplish a lot and reach their goals

- They manage people well

- They have control over their lives

- They keep their commitments

- They take an interest in others success

Why are successful people successful?
How do successful people become successful?

- Some people are just smarter...genetics does play a role,

- Some people are just luckier...we cannot wait for our luck to change,

- Some people work harder...and hard work usually pays off,

> *"THE HARDER I WORK,*
> *THE LUCKIER I GET."*
> *GARY PLAYER, GOLFER*

- Some people know how to work smarter.

Working smarter means managing your resources.
Time is a resource.

We All Waste Time!

There are not many things in life that are free, but time is truly free. We all have 24 hours a day. How we use it is our choice. If we use this resource properly we will accomplish the things that are important to us.

The problem is that some of us waste that time.

Research has shown:

- The average person loses **1 hour per day** due to disorganization.

    This equals 365 hours a year
    or 15.2 days every year

- The average person spends **28 minutes a day**, looking for things.

    This means 170 hours a year
    or 7 full days every year

Even if these figures are inflated by 50% the numbers are still staggering.

**Time wasted is a resource
you can never recover.**

Things That Waste Your Time

There are many things that waste your time and most of the time you are not fully aware it is happening. Can you relate to any of these? If so, there are things you can do.... Behavior you can change.

- **Interruptions:** Phone calls you accept when you are working on something very important and you don't even know who is calling.

- **Poor Planning:** Not anticipating time required to do a job thereby impacting other activities.

- **Incomplete Information:** Starting a project and realizing you don't have the information to finish.

- **Perfectionism:** Spending an inordinate amount of time to finish the final 5% of a project trying to make it 'perfect', instead of moving on.

- **Procrastination:** Delaying decisions.

- **Doing everything yourself:** Not delegating or asking for help.

- **Taking on too much:** Realizing later you cannot do everything.

- **Poor telephone etiquette**: Not leaving clear and concise voice messages resulting in phone tag.

- **Too much socializing:** (…enough said)

Signs Of Poor Time Management

There are many overt signs of poor time management and most of us do not always recognize them, let alone try to do anything about them.

- **Lateness**...always a sign of someone who cannot manage their time and does not respect other people's time.

- **Missing deadlines**...missing deadlines is a sure sign that someone did not plan ahead or organize their work.

- **Last minute**...always rushing to get things done at the last minute.

- **Lack of progress**...not being able to move forward with your work.

- **Lack of vision or focus**...not being clear why you are doing a task.

- **Lack of achievement**...never finishing or accomplishing tasks.

- **Frustration**...leading to mistakes.

- **Stress, irritability or being tired and unmotivated.**

- **Inferior quality** of work.

- **Difficult relationships** with friends and co-workers.

Your Personal Time Management

Here are some things you can do to help with your time management:

- **Plan your day.**
  At the end of the day look at the things you have accomplished and make a list of the things to be done the next day. Don't look at only your business activities, be sure to list the personal things in your life as well. Consider them in order of *importance* not *urgency*. Try establishing longer range goals and review them regularly.

- **Focus.**
  When you are working on any important project, concentrate on what you are doing. Try not to be distracted by unimportant activities and don't go from task to task without completing any. Stick with the top priorities until they are done.

- **Write things down.**
  It is impossible to remember everything you want to and forgetting to do things in a timely way is a major time waster and can have serious consequences. Use a journal, handheld or tablet to put down your thoughts and ideas regularly. Carry it with you and review it often.

- **Prioritize.**
  Doing the job *right* is not the goal, doing the right *job* is the goal. Priorities change on a regular basis so if you are not constantly reviewing and evaluating them you will have problems getting anything done.

- **Be realistic.**
It is human nature to underestimate the time for a job. We all want to please people but don't make a promise that you cannot keep. It is better to be open and honest early than having to make excuses after you are late.

- **Avoid procrastination.**
Procrastination by definition means to defer action or to delay. Nike's slogan has the right attitude. "Just Do It." Do it now and you won't have to remember to do it later. Make simple decisions by flipping a coin.

- **Be organized.**
Don't believe that a cluttered desk is the sign of a good worker. It's not! If you are not organized in you work you won't be organized in your thoughts and mistakes will be made. Be more organized than those you work with and you will eventually be running the show.

- **Be on time.**
Not being punctual is not only rude; it wastes the time of those kept waiting. It is a bad habit that can be cured. If you don't think it is important enough to arrive at a meeting on time, maybe you are not important enough to be in it. Better still...always arrive ahead of time. It is a lot less stressful on you and shows you are serious about what you are doing and your job.

- **Stay healthy.**
  Getting plenty of rest is not just a good idea, it is necessary if you are going to perform well at your job. Avoid fatigue so you can maintain your energy level. Your mind cannot concentrate if you are not rested and healthy.

- **Return phone calls.**
  Immediately. If you do so, you don't have to remember to do it later and you might eliminate a potential problem or better still, you might just open up a new opportunity.

> *"IMPORTANT PEOPLE*
> *RETURN PHONE CALLS.*
> *SELF-IMPORTANT PEOPLE DON'T."*
> *MARK WICKEN*

- **Meet deadlines.**
  Isn't it interesting that the word "deadlines" has the word *dead* in it? Probably for a reason. Keep important projects you are working on visible. Also keep deadlines in sight as a reminder.

- **Do it early rather that late.**
  If you have a small unpleasant task ahead, clear it off at the start of your day. This way you won't worry about it or be distracted the rest of your day anticipating doing it.

Chapter Summary

1. Time management is a skill that can only be learned with discipline and practice. Manage your time, don't waste it.

2. When people are good at what they do and happy with their lives it is usually because they are in control over their lives. Time management gives you that control.

3. Every employer wants an employee who can balance their time to accomplish all the things they need to be successful. Your business success will depend on how you balance the time in your life.

"TIME IS MORE VALUABLE THAN MONEY. YOU CAN ALWAYS GET MORE MONEY BUT YOU CANNOT GET MORE TIME."
JIM ROHN

Chapter 11

SUMMARY

*"HARD WORK DOESN'T GUARANTEE SUCCESS,
BUT IT IMPROVES ITS CHANCES."*
B.J. GUPTA

OPPORTUNITIES TO CREATE YOUR *"REMEMBER ME!"* IMPRESSIONS

By now you have read every chapter and should understand how your **"Remember Me!"** strategy works. It is the cumulative effect of every opportunity to leave the right impression that will make the real difference.

Here they are again...

Your Cover Letter.
Your cover letter is the first opportunity to tell the potential employer and decision-maker why he/she should consider looking at your resumé. It must be directed to the decision-maker. A good cover letter shows your professionalism, writing skills and enthusiasm for the job and company.

Your Resumé.
Your resumé must answer the employer's question: "Do I want to meet this person?" You must highlight your skills and accomplishments. A great resumé tells about your skills but, most importantly, what you have learned. What you have learned is what you bring to the job.

Your First Phone Contact.
Your phone call to confirm receipt of your resumé will be the first time the employer hears your voice. Calling off-hours and leaving a voice mail avoids the embarrassing moment that could occur if you call and the employer has not yet seen your resumé. You are calling to say "I will be calling...get ready." A clear concise message will convey to the employer you are professional, articulate, and motivated.

Your Phone Call To Set Up The Interview.
Once you finally speak to the decision-maker, have your opening "elevator speech" ready and ask to meet with them. If he/she indicates they are not hiring, remind them you have just graduated and ask if you could meet with them to get some help and/or direction with your chosen career.

Your Pre-Interview Phone Call.
Calling the day before the interview to confirm shows you are organized, enthusiastic, and it is one more time for the decision-maker to hear your voice before he/she actually meets you. Even if you only leave a voice-mail confirming your interview, it shows your professionalism and motivation.

Your First Impression.
Your attire, handshake, eye contact, your first words... all will be part of that important first impression. Appropriate dress and greetings will always indicate to the decision-maker that you are serious about the job. It shows you are a professional.

The First Five Minutes Of Your Interview.
With your opening remarks you can clearly establish you are enthusiastic, appreciative, determined and personable. Remember, the decision-maker hasn't asked you one question yet and he/she already has had a chance to draw conclusions about you from your actions and behavior. In the first five minutes the interviewer will make up his /her mind about your confidence, preparedness and motivation.

The Way You Answer The Interview Questions.
Being prepared to answer all interview questions is a given. Remember to respond as if the interviewer says after every question...."and what's in it for me?"
Answering in this way will show you are confident, informed and articulate. It also tells the interviewer you understand that you are being hired to work hard and make a contribution to the company.

The Great Questions You Ask About The Company.
By asking solid, well-informed questions about the company tells the interviewer you have done your research, you are interested, prepared and serious about the position.

Your Closing Speech.
Your closing…"I want this job" speech could be the deal maker. Finish the interview by telling the interviewer you want the job and the reasons why you know you are right for the job. This will show you are confident, assertive, determined and motivated. If you don't specifically ask for the job and tell them you want the job, why would you expect them to offer it to you?

Your "Thank-You" Follow-Up Contact.
Your "Thank-you" note or letter is one more opportunity to tell the interviewer why they should hire you and to tell them you want the job. Besides…it's good manners.

If you do not send a note, they may conclude you are not interested. A professional follow-up letter shows you are appreciative, professional, sincere, determined and says:

"I want this job!"

SEE EXHIBIT 9 FOR YOUR COMPLETE JOB-SEARCH CHECKLIST

APPENDIX

Exhibit 1
Your Cover Letter For Posted Positions

Date   Your Address

Name of Recipient
Title of Recipient
Address of Company

                              Re: Name of Position

Dear: (Mr. Mrs. Ms.)

    I am writing to express my interest in the current opening for a (position at company) advertised on ___?___.

As a recent graduate from ___?___ I believe my education, work experience and qualifications complement the responsibilities outlined in the advertisement (or job description). I've been able to advance my education and career through demonstrated initiative and the ability to work effectively under pressure. I am currently ___?___ and as you can see from my attached resumé, I have had extensive experience ___?___.

I am a motivated self starter, flexible team player with a friendly professional personality. I take pride in my work, have an excellent work ethic and possess a strong sense of responsibility. My part-time work in ____?____ has provided me with the tools to be an effective communicator with excellent interpersonal and organizational skills.

I believe my education, experience and skills make me a strong candidate for this position at ____?____. I look forward to an opportunity to meet with you so we can further discuss my qualifications.

Sincerely,
(signature)
Your Name

Exhibit 2
Your Cover Letter For "Cold-Calls"

Date

Your Address

Name of Recipient
Title of Recipient
Address of Company

Re: Name of Position

Dear: (Mr. Mrs. Ms.)

I am writing to express my interest in opportunities at (name of company) for an entry-level_____.

As you can see from my attached resumé, I recently graduated from (course and school). I believe my education, experience and qualifications make me a viable candidate to meet the challenges of a career in ___?___. I have been able to advance my education and career through demonstrated initiative and the ability to work effectively under pressure. I currently hold a position ____?____ and believe I have the knowledge and understanding of ____?____ necessary to make a meaning contribution to ___?____.

I am a motivated self-starter, flexible team player with a friendly professional personality. I take pride in my work, have an excellent work ethic and possess a strong sense of responsibility. My experience in ____?____ has provided me with the tools to be an effective communicator with excellent interpersonal and organizational skills.

I believe my experience and my diverse skills, make me a strong candidate for an entry-level position at ___?___.

I will contact you in the next few days to see if there is an opportunity to meet and discuss further. I look forward to speaking with you.

Sincerely,
(signature)
Your Name

Exhibit 3

Your Cover Letter Checklist

Every time you send out your cover letter and resumé, use this simple checklist to be sure it gets to the right person and gets your resumé read.

Recipient:

- ○ Have I addressed my letter to a specific person?
- ○ Have I confirmed the recipient's name, title, company and spelling?
- ○ Have I dated the letter?
- ○ Have I addressed the recipient properly (no first name) Mr. / Ms.?

Content:

- ○ Have I explained why I am writing and/or how I found out about the opportunity?
- ○ Have I stated my current situation (just graduated)?
- ○ Have I including at least one sentence that indicates I know something about the company?
- ○ Have I emphasized how my education and qualifications make me appropriate for the position?
- ○ Have I stated my resumé is enclosed or attached?
- ○ Have I made reference in the cover letter to something on my resumé that may be of interest to the employer?

Closing:

- ○ Have I requested the opportunity to meet with the employer to discuss the opportunity?
- ○ Have I expressed my enthusiasm for the opportunity?
- ○ Have I told the employer I will be calling them?
- ○ Have I signed the letter?

Overall:

- ○ Have I confirmed all the contact information?
- ○ Have I put my contact information on the letter?
- ○ Have I checked and double-checked spelling, grammar and punctuation?
- ○ Have I had someone else proof-read my cover letter?

☑ ...if so, I am ready to go.

Exhibit 4
Your Basic Resumé Format

YOUR NAME
123 Main Street
City, State/Province, Country, Zip/Postal
Home: (416) 555-5555 Mobile: (416) 555-5555
e-mail: yourname@abc.com
http://www.linkedIn.com/in/yourname

CAREER OBJECTIVE

A clear statement of who you are, what type of person you are and the type of position, work environment and challenge you are looking for.

PROFILE (optional)

Overview of who you are and what you have done

SUMMARY OF SKILLS

List specific skills that relate to your career objectives

EDUCATION

Institution (Degree / Courses)   Dates

EMPLOYMENT HISTORY
Company

Title/Position (Full or part-time)   Dates
Description of the company, type of business, service
Responsibilities:
Role within the company including whom you reported to
Skills Learned or Accomplishments:
Statement of performance, measurable/quantifiable

Company #2 etc. etc.

ACTIVITIES: List of non-work related activities, clubs, associations,

INTERESTS: List of personal interests, hobbies etc.

REFERENCES: Names provided: "Upon request"

Exhibit 5

Your Resumé Checklist

Before you send out your resumé, use this checklist to make sure you are not missing anything, and that everything is correct.

Objective:

- ○ Does my objective clearly state the position I am applying for?
- ○ Have I avoided using the words like "looking to get experience" in my objective?
- ○ Does my objective include the abilities specified by the employer in the job posting or abilities I know they are looking for?

Education:

- ○ Have I included my complete academic background with dates?
- ○ Have I included course work that support my objective?
- ○ Have I included my GPA?

Employment History or Work Experience:
(internship, co-op or part time)

- ○ Does each job listing contain the employer's name and type of business?
- ○ Does each job listing describe my responsibilities?
- ○ Does each job listing describe my accomplishments or the skills I learned from the experience?

Activities and Interests:

- ○ Have I included clubs, organizations or other activities that help describe the kind of person I am?
- ○ Have I included awards and special accomplishments?

Overall:

- ○ Is the design appealing, organized and easy to read?
- ○ Will my resumé reproduce correctly if photocopied?
- ○ Do I have an digital version if required?
- ○ Have I ensured the digital version transmits correctly?
- ○ Have I put my contact information on all pages?
- ○ Have I checked and double-checked spelling, grammar and punctuation?
- ○ Have I had someone else proof-read my resumé?

✓...if so, I am ready to go.

Exhibit 6
USE THIS FORM TO KEEP TRACK OF YOUR JOB-SEARCH CONTACTS

INFORMATION
Company Name:
_____

Contact Name/Title:
_____

Address:
_____

Phone or email:
_____

Company Information:
_____
_____
_____
_____
_____

Referred to by: (Name)
_____

Phone or email:
_____

CONTACTS:

Cover Letter and Resumé sent: (Date)
_____

Follow-up: (Date)
_____

Results: (Next Steps)
_____

_____

_____

Interview Date:
_____

Follow-ups:
_____

Next Steps:
_____

_____

_____

_____

Exhibit 7

Your Interview Checklist

As soon as you receive notification about your interview, here is a checklist to follow:

Pre-Interview:

- ○ Have I called to thank the caller and confirm the interview time, date, location and name of the interviewer?
- ○ Have I asked about parking, transit and where to enter the building?
- ○ Have I asked if there is a job description?

Days Before Interview:

- ○ Have I been on the company's web site?
- ○ Have I researched information about the job, company and interviewer?
- ○ Have I prepared my interview kit: resumé, references, portfolio? (if applicable)
- ○ Have I got my pad and pen ready?
- ○ Have I decided on my wardrobe?
- ○ Have I prepared my opening speech?
- ○ Have I prepared answers to every interview question I can think of?
- ○ Have I made my list of questions about the job and company?
- ○ Have I prepared my closing speech?
- ○ Have I called to confirm the interview the day before?
- ○ Will I get a good night's sleep before the interview?

Day Of Interview:

- Have I double-checked that I have all the things I need?
- Have I looked in the mirror? Do I look great?
- Do I have my "Thank-you" letter ready to finalize and send after the interview?
- Will I arrive at least 15 minutes early?
- Have I turned off my cell phone?
- Am I confident and smiling?

✓...if so, I am ready to go.

Exhibit 8
Here are some interview questions you should expect.

- Tell me about yourself.
- Who are you?
- Why are you interested in (Industry)?
- Why are you interested in this job? (this company?)
- What did you do to prepare for this interview?
- What would you like to know about the company?
- Why do you want to work here?
- What do you know about our company?
- What are your career goals?
- Where do you want to be in five years?
- What is your long-term career objective?
- How do you measure success?
- What motivates you?
- Describe the perfect job for you.
- What do you consider to be your biggest accomplishment?

More Questions...

- Tell me about your current job, or your last or your part-time job

- What do you feel you accomplished in your last job?

- What were your responsibilities in your last, part-time or summer job?

- Discuss any problems you might have had on any of your jobs.

- What disappointments, if any, have you had in your last job, part-time or summer job?

- What was a typical day on your previous job like?

- What did you like best about your last job, part-time or summer?

- What did you like least about your last job, part-time or summer?

- What are the reasons for leaving each of your previous jobs?

- What are your strengths?

- What are your weaknesses?

- What do you consider to be your greatest attribute and why?

More Questions…

- What are the areas you think you need to improve on?
- What are you looking for in this job you didn't have in your last job?
- What do you think you can bring to this job?
- What experience do you have that prepares you for this position?
- What are your interests outside of work?
- How do you think your family would describe you?
- How do you think your fellow students would describe you?
- Who influenced you most during your schooling years? In what way?
- What do you like to do in your spare time?
- If you could change one thing about yourself, what would it be?
- Why did you choose to go to the (school, college or university)?
- What courses did you like best? Why?
- What courses did you enjoy least? Why?

More Questions...

- What were your marks?

- If I were to ask your previous boss what he or she thought of you, what would he or she say?

- What is your salary in your present job?

- Do you feel you were being paid fairly?

- Can you delegate? Give me an example.

- What are your salary expectations? How have you arrived at this?

- Do you have any concerns about this job?

- Is there anything we haven't discussed that I should know about?

- Why should we hire you for this position?

- What do you think you can contribute to the company?

Remember, the key to answering all of these questions is to assume after every question the interviewer is saying..."and what's in it for me?"

Exhibit 9

YOUR JOB-SEARCH CHECKLIST
Prepared For Your Job Search?
This Is Your Checklist...Are You Ready?
(Rate your preparedness from 1 to 10)

Cover Letter
Not necessary   Targeted

1   2   3   4   5   6   7   8   9   10

Resumé
Have one that's OK   Current

1   2   3   4   5   6   7   8   9   10

References
Not yet   Have 3+

1   2   3   4   5   6   7   8   9   10

LinkedIn
Not on   Contacts 500+

1   2   3   4   5   6   7   8   9   10

Network List
Not yet   Have 20+

1   2   3   4   5   6   7   8   9   10

Target Companies
A few   Have 20+

1   2   3   4   5   6   7   8   9   10

Elevator Speech
What's that?   Know it by heart

1   2   3   4   5   6   7   8   9   10

Ready for Interview
I'll just "wing-it"   Have all the answers

1   2   3   4   5   6   7   8   9   10

"Thank-you" Letter
Not really important   Ready to go

1   2   3   4   5   6   7   8   9   10

"Attitude" Check
Scared to death   Excited to start

1   2   3   4   5   6   7   8   9   10

(100 out of 100 and You <u>ARE</u> ready)
Good Luck!

Exhibit 10

HARD TO BELIEVE?

For your fun and amusement, here are some of the interview mistakes graduates have made in the past.
(I DID NOT MAKE THIS STUFF UP.)

- Arriving late or on the wrong date
- Arriving one hour early
- Lighting up a cigarette in the interview
- Smelling like cigarettes
- Arriving right from the gym…hot and sweaty
- Arriving with a coffee in hand.(Why not bring one for the interviewer?)
- Eating and drinking in the reception area while waiting
- Putting on make-up in the reception area (ladies?)
- Talking on a cell phone in the reception area while the interviewer is waiting
- Putting feet up casually on the desk (honestly, it happened)
- Bad-mouthing previous bosses or jobs
- Lying or exaggerating about skills/experience/knowledge
- Wearing the wrong (for the workplace!) clothes

- Forgetting and mispronouncing the name of the interviewer
- Wearing too much perfume or aftershave
- Wearing sunglasses
- Wearing a Bluetooth earpiece
- Failing to do any research on the company in advance
- Failing to show any interest or enthusiasm
- Inquiring about benefits and salary
- Unable to explain how their strengths and abilities apply to the job
- Failing to able to articulate why they should be hired for this job
- Forgetting to bring a copy of their resumé and/or portfolio
- Failing to remember what was written on their resumé
- Asking too many questions
- Asking no questions at all
- Being unprepared to answer the basic interview questions
- Failing to listen to what the interviewer is asking
- Interrupting the interviewer
- Yawning
- Slouching

- Bringing along a friend to the interview (waiting outside)
- Chewing gum, tobacco, their pen, their hair
- Laughing, giggling, whistling, humming
- Continually saying "you know," "like," "right," and "um."
- Name-dropping, bragging or sounding like a know-it-all
- Asking to use the bathroom part way through the interview
- Shaking hands too weakly or too firmly
- Failing to make and keep continuous eye contact
- Taking a seat before the interviewer does
- Becoming angry or defensive about a question
- Complaining that they were kept waiting in the lobby
- Complaining about the weather…traffic….etc.!
- Speaking rudely to the receptionist
- Letting nervousness show
- Excuses about why they lost their last job, part-time..etc.
- Being too casual, familiar and trying to be funny
- Sounding desperate
- Checking their watch in the interview
- Sounding rehearsed
- Leaving their cell phone on

- Asking the interviewer for a ride home after the interview
- Answering a cell phone call and asking the interviewer to leave the room because it was private (really!)
- Brushing hair before the interview started
- Saying he or she was not really a "people person"
- Arriving smelling of alcohol
- Flushing the toilet while talking during a phone interview (honest!)
- Trying to tell a joke
- Failing to tell the interviewer they wanted the job
- Failing to say "thank-you" after the interview
- No follow-up after the interview

> **"WE LEARN BY OUR MISTAKES BUT, A WISE PERSON LEARNS BY THE MISTAKES THAT HAVE BEEN MADE BY OTHERS."**
> **DAI VERNON**

Myths & Realities Of Your Job Search

Myths & Realities
Of Your Job Search

In the job-search world, there are many misconceptions. Here are some common myths and realities surrounding resumés, cover letters, and job interviews.

****

Myth: Describe your ideal job in your resumé objective or cover letter so hiring managers can determine if you will be happy with the job.

Reality: The employer isn't interested in what makes you happy. They want to know how you will make them happy and contribute to their company's goals and objectives. Use your objective to introduce yourself and indicate how your education, experience, and skills will bring value to the employer. Remember, your resumé is a marketing tool and the objective must address their needs…not yours.

****

Myth: Your resumé should give all the details about all your part-time and summer work experience to convince the employer to hire you.

Reality: Your resumé is supposed to get you an interview, not a *job*. It should give relevant information and skills you have learned from your previous experience that are applicable to the job you are applying for.

****

Myth: An elaborate resumé design with cool fonts will stand out from the crowd and get attention.

Reality: If you are applying for a position within a creative industry, design will certainly be under scrutiny. Your resumé layout should be professional and visually pleasing. It is important that your resumé be clear enough to be readable when copied, faxed or emailed. Don't let your design get in the way of communication.

****

Myth: Networking ends when the meeting or event is over.

Reality: Networking is the beginning of a relationship. After you have met a person, your follow-up behavior (phone call, email, etc.) will develop and maintain the relationship if you do it properly and with respect.

****

Myth: The employer will be smart enough to realize that your experience is very close to what they're looking for, just by reading your resumé.

Reality: Often, the first "reader" of your resumé may be a software application programmed to scan resumés. Specific resumés with high keyword counts usually get read. If there is a job description, look at it for keywords and customize your resumé to each employer's wording.

****

Myth: Nobody reads cover letters anymore. Why send one?

Reality: It's true that some hiring managers don't read cover letters, but most still do (at some point). A well-written cover letter serves as the introduction to your resumé, highlighting your strengths and reasons to look at your resumé, which in turn can lead to an interview. A cover letter is also a writing sample that shows off your communication skills. It can also show you know something about the company. Even if no one reads it, the fact that you bothered to write a cover letter gives the impression that you pay attention to detail and you are professional. There is no downside to sending a cover letter with your resumé.

****

Myth: Studying the company's web site is good preparation for the interview.

Reality: That's just the beginning. Don't just look at it. See what the company is all about, the players, their customers and competitors. Read the annual report, their blog and press releases. Do your research and you'll have an advantage, because most first-time job seekers don't bother to go that far.

****

Myth: When asked about salary over the phone, you should lowball them to get the interview.

Reality: If you're asked for a salary range, be truthful.

****

Myth: In a job interview, the interviewer is in control.

Reality: You give an interview; you do not take an interview. It should be a two-way exchange. In a good interview, you should ask as many questions as the interviewer asks, if not more. You can show that you've done your research by asking questions about the company. Remember this is "your" interview and it is your job to leave the interviewer with the right impression about you. You cannot do that if you don't make sure you tell them all the things about you that make you suitable for the position.

****

Myth: The first thing you should ask about is salary and benefits, because if they're too low, there's no point in wasting your time.

Reality: This is always the question most graduates wrestle with. Remember, this is an entry-level job, your first. The employer knows exactly what they are going to pay you, so it is not a guessing game or a negotiation. You should probably have some idea about salary levels before you apply, but remember, you do not have much to negotiate with. What you really want is the opportunity to show them you can do the job.

****

Myth: The most qualified, most experienced, and most educated candidate always gets the job.

Reality: Getting hired is a matter of presenting yourself as the best solution to the employer's problem or need. Convince them that you've got the right skills, the right attitude, and the right stuff to solve their problems, and you will get the job. Remember, it is usually the person who does the best job of interviewing who gets the job.

****

Myth: Your resumé should indicate you're great at everything.

Reality: Have you ever seen a job posting that said, "We want to hire someone who's good at everything"? People get hired to do specific tasks with specific skills and specific duties. If your resumé says, "I can do everything"... No one will believe you..plain and simple....you cannot do everything. Your resumé should support your marketable strengths and transferable skills. Tell them what have you learned?

****

Myth: If the job posting says "No Calls," you should call anyway…it will show that you're really interested.

Reality: If they say don't call, don't call. If you try, you are telling them you cannot read or cannot follow instructions. This is the best way to make a bad first impression.

****

Myth: The more jobs you apply for, the better your chances of getting that first job.

Reality: Targeted approaches to your job search are the ones that will work. You learn more and get better at your approach if you really understand the companies to which you are applying. Do not apply everywhere. The best strategy is to take a marketing approach to each job opportunity with a targeted letter. A customized resumé that shows your skills as they relate to the job's requirements is the best way to secure an interview.

****

Myth: Put as much information on your resumé as you can.

Reality: If your resumé includes details for every job you have ever held, your resumé is too long. The best resumés are targeted, concise and specific. Two pages maximum… highlighting responsibilities, accomplishments and skills learned.

****

Myth: In a cover letter, you should quote from the job posting.

Reality: Don't copy words directly from the job posting, but address the points in your cover letter with specific examples that address the points on the job description.

****

Myth: You don't need a "summary" or "profile" section on your resumé.

Reality: A summary or profile on your resumé is an absolutely critical element, as it ties together what you've done. A well-written summary or profile demonstrates your writing skills and states why they should want to meet you.

****

Myth: When it comes to networking, call, connect or get together with everyone you can.

Reality: Use new technologies, especially social networks, to spread the word, but use them strategically. Remember employers use them too.

****

Myth: A resumé is an historical document for the record.

Reality: Your resumé is not a self-validating document. It is an advertisement about you, highlighting your strengths and what you can offer. It must show your potential and indicate to the employer what you can do for them if they hire you.

****

Myth: Follow-up only once or twice after an interview.

Reality: Timing is everything, and if you are sending professional emails with good thoughts they will perceive you are organized, persistent and enthusiastic. If you don't follow-up, they may conclude you are not or are no longer interested. Follow-up is critical to your success.

****

Myth: References from former employers can only confirm employment.

Reality: References are important and can make or break the decision to hire you. Treat them with care and respect, and always call to thank your reference after they have been called. It is the polite and right thing to do.

****

Myth: Responding to a posted position is the best way to get a job.

Reality: If responding to a "corporate" posted position, your odds of getting an interview are, at best, 1 in 10. Your best strategy is to look for the hidden job market by doing your research and networking effectively.

****

Myth: The "Big" job boards have the most openings.

Reality: Only 30% of jobs at major companies are listed on big job boards. Most companies use networking, internal postings and their own sites to avoid the rising costs of screening resumés.

Myth: Internet technology makes landing a job easier.

Reality: The Internet is a research tool. The Internet best identifies opportunities rather than serving as a vehicle to apply for a job. Networking and employee referrals are the #1 source of new hires for most companies.

****

Myth: Using Internet technology will help differentiate you from your competition.

Reality: Hardly. The Internet does not eliminate competition, but can help you stay ahead of the competition. The Internet will not make your job search easy...it might make it easier. It will not differentiate you from your competitors.

****

Myth: Social networks are not important.

Reality: Social networks are part of our lives now. If not used properly, they can be dangerous. Social and professional networks are more connected than ever and will grow. Social networks can give you control over your message, if used correctly. If you do not control what is out there about you, it could send the wrong message. Employers check Facebook. Most employers will do background checks on candidates they are interested in, just to see what they find. If they find something that puts doubt in their minds... you lose.

****

Myth: One resumé works for all opportunities.

Reality: Your resumé must relate to the job opportunity. The reader must say...."I want to meet this person." Therefore, your resumé must be targeted to the recipient in order to draw attention to the points you have determined will be the most relevant to the employer.

****

Myth: Interviewers care about your long-term objectives.

Reality: Interviewers only care about hiring the right person to fill the position…their job often depends on it. Your long-term objectives should be associated with doing a good job for the employer and making a meaningful contribution to the company.

****

Myth: Companies hire the most qualified candidate.

Reality: Companies hire the person they determine is the best fit for the position and company.

****

Myth: "Thank-you" notes are passé, "old school" and not necessary.

Reality: "Thank-you" notes give you one more opportunity to tell the interviewer why they should hire you…and besides, it good manners. If you don't send one, they may conclude you are no longer interested. There is no downside to sending a "Thank-you" note or letter.

****

Myth: It's not *who* you know, it's *what* you know.

Reality: Network, network, network… "Good people know good people."

****

Myth: Showing up at a company, unannounced, a "cold call" is a good way to show you are confident and assertive.

Reality: Are you nuts? Bad idea!! People with jobs are usually working when you show up. They are unprepared to meet you, and probably won't have time. You have "invaded their space" without their permission.....Is this a great "first impression?"...No!. There is a good chance it will create a bad first impression.

****

Myth: Get your resumé in front of the human resources manager first.

Reality: Failing to follow instructions will only irritate the hiring manager. If you are applying to a posted position, follow instructions exactly. If you are applying on a "cold call" basis check out their web site for the name of the most appropriate person to approach.

****

Myth: Resumés or cover letters with typos or grammatical errors are no big deal...mistakes happen.

Reality: Wrong! If the hiring person is looking for a way to eliminate candidates, you just gave it to them. This is a no-brainer...all it says is you are careless and unprofessional.

****

Myth: If there are gaps in your resumé (such as travel), you can always explain it to them in the interview.

Reality: A gap in your resumé raises a question..what happened? You might not get the interview to explain. A gap could suggest a potential problem or mystery. Tell the truth and/or explain it in the cover letter. Gaps for travel could be a good thing. I could tell the employer you have travel "out of your system" and are now ready to apply yourself to your career.

****

Myth: Tell the employer what you did in your part-time, internship or summer job.

Reality: The employer is not interested in what you did...they are interested in what you can do for them. So tell them what you have "learned" in you part-time, internship or summer job. What you have learned is what you will bring to the job.

****

Myth: Apply for jobs you are under-qualified for and hope you can impress them in the interview.

Reality: If you are under-qualified, you probably won't get an interview. So don't waste your time and that of the employer. Be realistic.

****

Myth: Using gimmicks or props to get the attention of the employer is a great way to make a first impression.

Reality: Stop! Think about it. If it is a brilliant "idea" you might be right. But if it is the wrong idea, you just might ruin an introduction and opportunity. Be careful, creative and professional...not silly and childish.

****

Myth: Today, more than ever, job-hunting online is the best route to go.

Reality: People hire people...face-to-face networking and contact is the best way to get people to know you. Online...you look like everyone else.

****

Myth: Good grades are the most important qualifications in your job search.

Reality: Most employers will tell you they look for a well-rounded graduate with not only good grades but one who is active in the community, does volunteer work and participates in extra-curricular activities.

****

Myth: Networking is selling.

Reality: Networking is marketing. When you are networking, you are building your connections…people who know you. Networking is a long-term strategy, not a quick-fix to satisfy a short-term need.

****

Myth: Employers only hire the best qualified candidates. Therefore inexperienced graduates do not stand a chance in a competitive market.

Reality: For entry-level positions, qualifications usually are limited to your education. Personal traits such as confidence, good manners, enthusiasm, honesty....these can be measured in an interview. You represent "potential" to the employer. Because you do not have any practical experience, you must win them over with your potential.

****

Myth: Using contacts or connections should be avoided in the cover letter or interview.

Reality: If you know or can be recommended by someone the employer knows and trusts, your chance of getting the interview or the job will be higher than someone without any connections.

****

Myth: Networking is telling people all about you.

Reality: Networking is about communicating and communicating is a two-way street. Listen more…talk less. We have two ears and one mouth…use them in this proportion. Use your elevator speech to introduce yourself and then listen.

****

Myth: Internet technologies make landing a job easier.

Reality: Research is research and the Internet is an excellent way to get information fast. As a place to find job opportunities, the Internet is just like any other place where jobs are posted. Thousands will see it and hundreds will apply. Think about the odds.

****

Myth: Social networks are different from professional networks.

Reality: Social media provide many ways to get information about people and companies. The problem with social media is that once information is out there, you cannot control it or withdraw it. Employers use social media sites when checking out potential employees. Be sure you don't put information (or pictures) on the Internet that you will regret.

****

Bibliography

There are many books that have helped me over the years and many have helped develop the job-search strategies contained in this book. Here are just a few I have referred to and consulted. I suggest you consider reading them.

How to Win Friends and Influence People:
by Dale Carnegie

Dig Your Well Before You're Thirsty:
by Harvey MacKay

Tapping The Iceberg:
by Tim Cork

The Intentional Networker:
by Patti DeNucci

At Ease...Professionally:
by Hilka Klinkenberg

Winning Body Language:
by Mark Bowden

The Unwritten Rules of the Highly Effective Job Search:
by Orville Pierson

Where Have I Gone Right?
by Jim Hayhurst Sr.

The Unofficial Guide to Landing a Job:
by L. Michelle Tullier

What Does Somebody Have To Do To Get A Job Around Here?
by Cynthia Shapiro

Don't Send A Resume:
by Jeffrey J. Fox

Your Career. How To Make It Happen:
by Julie Griffin Levitt

About Mark Wicken

Mark is an educator and marketing professional with more than 35 years of marketing, advertising and communications experience in the United States, Canada and the Middle East.

He has held senior account management positions with several multi-national advertising agencies and has been responsible for accounts including IBM, Esso, McDonald's, and General Motors.

He was Divisional Vice President of Marketing for Canada with Domino's Pizza International as well as Director of Marketing for KFC restaurants in the Middle East.

Mark successfully transferred his experience into executive search, and established The Mark Wicken Group, a business specializing in executive search within the marketing, advertising and communications industries. Mark also teaches job search, presentation skills, resumé writing and interviewing skills.

Mark has devoted much of his life to teaching, education and youth development, and is currently President of MusicFest Canada, the largest annual education-based music festival in North America. He has also been an instructor in marketing, business, career planning and job search at several colleges, universities and private institutions.

Mark understands job search, the hiring process and the obstacles every new graduate faces as they move into the business world. As a business professional, educator and executive recruiter Mark has studied all aspects of the job-search process as it pertains to new graduates. He has written this book to address the specific needs of those entering the job market for the first time.

THE LAST WORDS

I have been conducting seminars and teaching job search to graduating students for many years. At the end of every course or session, I give each student a button that says, **"Remember Me!"** *I hope this will be a reminder throughout their job search to look for ways that will create those* **"Remember Me!"** *moments for the employers they approach and the people they meet. If you see someone with one of these buttons, ask them how their* **"Remember Me!"** *job-search strategy worked for them.*

…(it's called networking.)

Good luck!

> "PEOPLE WILL FORGET WHAT YOU SAID.
> PEOPLE WILL FORGET WHAT YOU DID.
> BUT PEOPLE WILL NEVER FORGET
> HOW YOU MADE THEM FEEL."
> MAYA ANGELOU